W9-CIQ-722

The IEA Health and Welfare Unit

Choice in Welfare No. 9

Empowering the Parents:
How to Break the
Schools Monopoly

Empowering the Parents: How to Break the Schools Monopoly

David G. Green (Editor)
Antony Flew
Julian Le Grand
Marjorie Seldon
David Robinson
Roy Carr-Hill

London
IEA Health and Welfare Unit
1991

First published in 1991
by
The IEA Health and Welfare Unit
2 Lord North St
London SW1P 3LB

ISBN 0-255 36270-6

Typeset by the IEA Health and Welfare Unit
Printed in Great Britain by
Goron Pro-Print Co. Ltd
Churchill Industrial Estate, Lancing, West Sussex

Contents

Acknowledgement

I would particularly like to take this opportunity to thank members of the Advisory Council of the Health and Welfare Unit for their hard work in reading and commenting on manuscripts. It has been a great advantage to be able to rely on such high quality advice and I cannot express my thanks strongly enough.

It goes without saying that the views expressed in *Empowering the Parents* are the authors' and not necessarily those of the IEA, its Advisers or Trustees.

David Green

The Authors

Antony Flew is Emeritus Professor of Philosophy in the University of Reading, and has for the last six years served for one semester a year as a Distinguished Research Fellow in the Social Philosophy and Policy Centre, Bowling Green State University, Ohio. He is a Charter Member of the Council of the Freedom Association and a member of the Education Group of the Centre for Policy Studies.

His books include: *Sociology, Equality and Education,* (1976); *The Politics of Procrustes: Contradictions of Enforced Equality,* (1981); *Thinking about Social Thinking,* (1984); *David Hume: Philosopher of Moral Science,* (1986); *Power to the Parents: Reversing Educational Decline,* (1987); and *Equality in Liberty and Justice,* (1989). There have also been pamphlets for the Institute of Economic Affairs, Centre for Policy Studies and the Social Affairs Unit, as well as numerous articles in the philosophers' trade journals.

Marjorie Seldon has been involved in voluntary work for the disabled as well as developments in education for much of her life. She was Founder Chairman of Friends of the Education Voucher Experiment (FEVER), is a member of the Education Group at the Centre for Policy Studies and Vice-Chairman of the National Education Committee. In 1989 she was invited by the New Zealand High Commissioner to participate in the special conference on lessons of British education for New Zealand. As well as being involved in numerous broadcasts she has written extensively on government and public policy aspects of education. Her publications include chapters in *The Right to Learn,* (1985); *British Education in the 1990s,* (1989); *Universities in the Modern World,* (1990). Her many articles have appeared in *Education, Economic Affairs, Independent Schools Information Service, The Free Trader, Crossbow, The New Outlook,* the *Daily Telegraph* and *The Sunday Times.* She is joint author of *The Education Voucher System,* an explanatory handbook.

Julian Le Grand is Professor of Public Policy at, and Director of, the School for Advanced Urban Studies at the University of Bristol. He is also co-director of the Welfare State Programme at the Suntory-Toyota International Centre for Economics and Related Disciplines, London School of Economics. He was previously a lecturer in economics at the University of Sussex and the London School of Economics. His books include *The Economics of Social Problems*, (with R. Robinson, Macmillan, 1984); *The Strategy of Equality*, (Allen and Unwin, 1982); *Not Only the Poor*, (with R. Goodin *et al.*, Allen and Unwin 1987); *Market Socialism*, (ed. with S. Estrin, Oxford University Press, 1989); and *Equity and Choice*, (Routledge, 1991). He has also published extensively in economics and other academic journals. He has acted as a consultant to the OECD, the French Government and the European Commission. He is currently a member of the Research Grants Board of the Economic and Social Research Council, and of the Avon Family Health Service Authority.

David Robinson is Professor of Health Studies and Pro-Vice-Chancellor at the University of Hull. He is also Director of the World Health Organisation Collaborating Centre for Research and Training in Psychosocial and Economic Aspects of Health. With Professor Alan Maynard he co-directed the Economic and Social Research Council's Addiction Research Centre from 1983-1988. Among his numerous books are *From Drinking to Alcoholism*, (1976); *Patients, Practitioners and Medical Care*, (1978); *Self-Help and Health*, (with Stuart Henry, 1977); *Preventing Alcohol Problems*, (with Philip Tether, 1986); *Controlling Legal Addictions*, (ed. with Alan Maynard and Robert Chester, 1989); and *Manipulating Consumption*, (ed. with Christine Godfrey, 1990). In January 1992 Professor Robinson takes up the position of Vice-Chancellor of the University of South Australia.

Roy Carr-Hill is Research Co-ordinator in the School of Social and Political Science at the University of Hull. Prior to this he held the posts of Senior Research Fellow in the Centre for Health Economics at York University from 1984-1991 and Research

Statistician in the Medical Research Council's Medical Sociology Unit at Aberdeen University from 1981-1983. Dr Carr-Hill has extensive experience as a regular consultant with the World Health Organisation, OECD, UNESCO and the Swedish International Development Agency. His books include *Crime, Police and Criminal Statistics*, (with Nick Stern, 1979); *The Development and Exploitation of Empirical Birthweight Standards*, (with C.W. Pritchard, 1985) and *Britain's Black Population: A New Perspective* (ed. with A. Bhat and S. Ohri, 1989).

Dr David G. Green is currently the Director of the Health and Welfare Unit at the Institute of Economic Affairs. He was formerly a Labour councillor in Newcastle upon Tyne from 1976 until 1981, and from 1981 to 1983 was a Research Fellow at the Australian National University in Canberra. He is the author of several articles on politics and social policy and his books include *Power and Party in an English City* (Allen & Unwin, 1980), *Mutual Aid or Welfare State* (Allen & Unwin, 1984) (with L. Cromwell), *Working Class Patients and the Medical Establishment* (Temple Smith/Gower, 1985), *Challenge to the NHS* (IEA, 1986), *The New Right: The Counter Revolution in Political, Economic and Social Thought* (Wheatsheaf, 1987), *Everyone a Private Patient* (IEA, 1988), and *Equalizing People* (IEA, 1990).

Editor's Introduction
Lessons From America?

David G. Green

From time to time, the education voucher has been declared dead by governments. But it refuses to die. Not only does the idea refuse to go away, it is gaining ground particularly on the left both in Britain and especially America.

Under the Citizen's Charter parents are to enjoy new rights to comparative information about schools. The wider disclosure of information is undoubtedly a step in the right direction, but evidence from overseas suggests that unless it is supplemented by other measures the gains will be limited.

Experience of reform in America during the past decade indicates that the education system cannot be radically improved unless two steps are taken to break the monopoly character of government schools. First, on the demand side, parents must be empowered through vouchers or scholarships so that their choices count. Second, the supply side should be de-regulated to allow the founding of new schools to shake the complacency of the education establishment.

The first essay in this volume is by the distinguished philosopher, Professor Antony Flew, who is concerned that education writers are squeamish about describing the education service as a monopoly when that is what it is. He represents local education authorities as monopoly suppliers of education to captive consumers with all that this entails for the inefficiency of the service. To emphasise the point, he re-names them 'local education monopolies'.

Marjorie Seldon, a tireless campaigner for educational reform, believes that the remedy is to introduce a voucher scheme to alter the balance of power in favour of parents, a view shared by professor Julian Le Grand, who writes from a socialist standpoint. His voucher scheme, however, contains an egalitarian element to mitigate the disadvantages of being born into a poor family.

Tried and Failed?

Whenever vouchers are advocated, a frequent response is that pilot schemes have been tried and the idea found wanting. The Kent County Council voucher proposal has gone down in anti-voucher mythology as a failed experiment. In fact it was a feasibility study of a pilot scheme which was not implemented because obstacles were put in its way by opponents at the Department of Education and Science and by the local teachers' unions. The experiment at Alum Rock in America is also frequently mentioned as having failed, but it was a very limited affair which was inconclusive.[1]

Fortunately, Kent and Alum Rock do not exhaust the repertoire of examples we can turn to for solid evidence of how a voucher scheme might turn out. First, as Professor Robinson and Roy Carr-Hill of Hull University argue in this volume, we can learn something from higher education. About one-third of the income of universities comes in the form of per capita payments for each student enroled and so if the fears of the critics of school voucher schemes were justified similar effects would be revealed in higher education. David Robinson and Roy Carr-Hill examine how this partial voucher scheme has worked and conclude that the lesson from higher education is that schools have little to fear from vouchers.

But most important of all, there have been several experiments in American schools. They were not always called voucher schemes, no doubt because the concept has become something cf a *bête noire*, but the experiments were voucher schemes in all but name. The most radical was attempted in East Harlem from 1974 onwards.[2]

3

Demand-Side Empowerment or Supply-Side De-Regulation

The traditional reasoning behind vouchers is straightforward. Education standards are believed to be too low because education is provided by local public-sector monopolies which are insufficiently concerned with parents' presumed preferences for high standards. The remedy, so the argument runs, is to put the consumer in the driving seat by allocating parents a voucher sufficient in value to buy education in a school of their choice for each of their children. This empowerment of parents will stimulate competition. Schools which attract parental support will flourish; and those which are unresponsive to parents' preferences will fail to attract pupils and will find it necessary to mend their ways or close.

The details vary, but under the simplest form of voucher scheme each year the government makes available to all children a voucher which represents the cash equivalent of educating a child of a given age for 12 months. The school chosen by the parents is then entitled to receive the cash equivalent of the voucher from the government. Other schemes, including one advocated by Professor Le Grand in this volume, add to the basic idea an element of equalization. In his scheme, children in low-income neighbourhoods would be given vouchers with a higher cash value to make up for the poverty of their home background.

Both the traditional voucher, inspired by classical liberalism, and the egalitarian variant focus on the demand side. They put their faith in the enfranchisement of parents as the mechanism that will stimulate change on the supply side. But more recent work in America casts doubt on the thesis that demand-side empowerment will be sufficient. In a study published by the leftist Brookings Institution, John Chubb and Terry Moe[3] urge radical supply-side de-regulation to break the stranglehold of central authority and to re-energise the idealism of teachers. The Brookings study is one of the most significant contributions to the debate about educational standards for many years and for that reason it is worthwhile pausing to review its arguments and to compare their relevance to recent developments in Britain.

Learning from American Mistakes

First, Chubb and Moe assess the effectiveness of the reforms which have been attempted in America in recent years. Significantly, they resemble recent British measures introduced following the 1988 Education Reform Act. They identify two waves of reforms. The first wave launched direct attacks on what appeared to be the problems: lack of resources, poor academic standards and inadequate teacher pay. These reforms tended to centralise decision-making power by adding to the regulations governing schools and school districts (the nearest equivalent to our local authorities). The second wave of reforms was based on the perception that excessive centralisation and bureaucracy were not the solution, but part of the problem. Consequently, the decentralisation of decision making to schools was urged, along with greater teacher professionalism and enhanced parental choice.

Centralising Decision Making: More Money and Controls

The reforms which had a centralising effect are divided into two categories: more money and more controls.

Drawing on numerous other studies and on their own work, Chubb and Moe's conclusion is that giving a school more money will not necessarily improve its performance. Schools that produce good academic results, measured by America's standardised Scholastic Aptitude Test (SAT), do have about 20 percent more resources on average than low-performing schools. But when adjustments are made for variables like social class, and student aptitude, this apparent causal connection breaks down. Moreover, private schools spend less per head than public schools and perform better. Money, Chubb and Moe conclude, 'is not what makes some schools more effective than others'. They summarise their argument thus:

> In our view, the performance problems of the public schools have little or nothing to do with inadequate funding, and they cannot be corrected by digging deeper into the public purse.[4]

A variety of measures have been introduced in America during the 1970s and 1980s to tackle low achievement, including reforms to introduce more control of discipline, the curriculum, teaching personnel, textbooks, and methods of teaching. A particularly common approach, which mirrors the British Government's introduction of national tests, was the requirement that schools introduce new formal tests of pupil performance to enable parents to see how well their children were doing and to assess the effectiveness of the school. Chubb and Moe have three main criticisms of uniform testing.

First, they are concerned that the tests measure only a part of what children learn, and that they do so imperfectly. Second, teachers will tend to 'teach to the tests' regardless of their real value in raising understanding. And third, test scores are in part the result of the school's input but also the result of home background, student attitude, social class, and other factors. Consequently, test results are not a failsafe indicator of the contribution the school has made to a child's performance.

These difficulties are well known and the authors conclude, that testing is desirable regardless of these flaws. However, they insist that the imposition of uniform tests may also do harm partly by diverting attention from the pursuit of higher quality and, in part, by leading to the introduction of additional bureaucracy. The danger, they say, 'is not just that these reforms will fail to accomplish their lofty goals, but that they will actually hurt the schools more than help them over the long run.'[5] The real challenge, they insist, is how to inspire teachers to greater efforts. Uniform testing regimes may compel teachers' formal compliance, and where there is an educational vacuum, this may do more good than harm, but testing alone cannot stimulate the willing enthusiasm of teachers. Indeed, the imposition of tests from above reinforces the subordinate status of teachers, which may make the task of altering their motivation more difficult.

Decentralising Reforms: Local Management and Parental Choice

The second wave of reforms emphasised the decentralisation of decision making. Two such measures resemble recent British reforms.

Some American reformers have argued that central regulation has failed and urge instead the liberation of schools from the straitjacket of bureaucratic control. The common result of such thinking has been the decentralisation of decision making to schools. School districts continue to make general policy, whilst individual schools control detailed implementation and enjoy a greater say in the disposal of their own budget.

Chubb and Moe's assessment of the local management of schools in America is that it is a step in the right direction, but that it has not led to fundamental change. The school district (the equivalent of the British local authority) remains ultimately responsible and if schools act controversially then the higher authority tends to step in. The schools enjoy autonomy, but only for the time being and when the going gets rough, their authority is soon curtailed. According to Chubb and Moe, it is an unstable arrangement: 'As long as higher-level authority exists, it will eventually get used.'[6]

Thus, American experience suggests that decentralisation has its place, but reforms rarely go far enough. It is too early to draw firm conclusions about British experience of local management of schools, but all the indicators are that the outcome will be the same. A useful dispersal of decision making will take place, but there will be no dramatic transformation of educational practice.

In the view of the Brookings study, the most innovative and most promising reforms have provided greater parental choice of school. Significantly, they report that in America schemes based on choice are not seen as right-wing devices for privatising all schools. The widening of choice attracts support from liberals and conservatives alike primarily because it is a device for reforming the schools whilst keeping them public. It is a strategy for reform from within the public sector. In some localities it has also formed a major part of programmes to combat racial segregation, including Rochester and Buffalo (New York), Cambridge (Massachusetts), and Prince George's County (Maryland).

Chubb and Moe strongly favour increased parental choice, but identify three basic weaknesses of the measures introduced so far. First, they report that the apparently wide support in America for choice is often very shallow. When discussion turns to details, support often breaks down.

Second, choice schemes focus on demand, that is parents have a choice of school, but only rarely is the supply side de-regulated in order to encourage the emergence of new and innovative schools. The parents' choice is usually restricted to existing schools which, it is hoped, will respond to competition. But these schools have their funds and their existence guaranteed and, precisely because they cannot go out of business, Chubb and Moe do not believe that enhanced parental choice alone can deliver vigorous competition.

The third defect of choice schemes is that any measure which upsets the traditional structure generates intense opposition with the result that programmes are usually a compromise between the vested interests:

> Choice becomes part of a big compromise among contending political powers—no one loses jobs, no bad schools are closed down, vested interests remain securely vested, the basic structure stays the same. In a nutshell, this is why reforms always focus on giving parents and students choice, but never free up the supply and governance of schools.[7]

Minnesota provides an example. It's scheme is among the broadest in scope of the open-enrolment experiments. Children can attend schools outside their own district with public money following their parents' choice. The results have been good but limited in scope because, as a result of the absence of supply-side deregulation, all the traditional institutions have remained in place.[8]

Some choice schemes have included 'magnet' schools similar to British city technology colleges. According to Chubb and Moe, magnet schools have proved successful for their own pupils, primarily because they are volunteers. Sometimes such schools have also had a limited rebound effect on nearby schools, but for the most part they have not been able to galvanise other schools into reform. This can only be accomplished, argue Chubb and Moe, if every school is a chosen school.

In America, magnet schools have often been an instrument of racial integration, based on the hope that through choice racial balance will be achieved, a strategy that has frequently worked. One of the bolder experiments of this type began in Cambridge, Massachusetts in the late 1960s but the initial results of relying on magnet schools were not wholly satisfactory and new reforms were introduced from 1981. Under that scheme, which is still in force, there are no neighbourhood schools and no catchment areas. Children can attend any school chosen by their parents, with the help of a parent information centre. Parents select up to four schools in order of priority and, based partly on their preferences and partly on each school's racial balance, their children are assigned to a school. Cambridge was a fortunate location for the experiment because there was already a degree of variation between schools, each with a different appeal. The consequence has been that the majority of children obtain their first choice, and almost all receive one of their first four selections.

The results have been promising: SAT scores in Cambridge are up, and the gap between the worst schools and the best schools has narrowed. Teachers are more satisfied with their work and parents with the results. Significantly, public schools are winning back pupils from the private sector: in 1979 the public sector had 78 per cent of all pupils, in 1987 it had 89 per cent.[9]

The weakness of the scheme is that the supply side remains under the control of the public authorities, and all the good that has been done could easily be reversed. According to Chubb and Moe, the value of de-regulating the supply side is demonstrated by the most radical and the most promising of all schemes so far, in East Harlem, New York.

Supply-Side De-Regulation in East Harlem

In 1973, out of 32 schools districts in New York, East Harlem was last in reading and maths. Poverty was widespread, with some 80 per cent of pupils receiving free lunches and more than half the families headed by lone females. The racial mix was 60 per cent Hispanic and 35 per cent black.

It was probably desperation that led school district leaders to attempt such a radical reform but it is fortunate for all parents that their experience can now be emulated. From 1974 the supply side was reformed. Teachers were encouraged to put forward their own proposals for new schools and instead of being centred on a building, schools were to be built around themes, programmes and philosophies. Each school would also control its own admissions and curriculum. Parents were to have complete choice of school within the district and money would follow their choice. Parents were encouraged to participate in their school and to feel a real sense of ownership. No less important, when schools failed to attract pupils they were to be closed.

The scheme has functioned since 1974 and the results have been dramatic. Schools proliferated, specialising in a wide variety of subjects, as the following examples testify: the Academy of Environmental Science, the Creative Learning Community, East Harlem Career Academy, East Harlem Maritime School, East Harlem School for Health and Biomedical Studies, the Jose Feliciano Performing Arts School, and the Isaac Newton School for Math and Science.

The outcome has not been chaos and unfairness as some predicted. About 60 per cent of children receive their first choice, 30 per cent their second choice, and five per cent their third choice. Student achievement is up. In 1973, only 15.9 per cent of pupils were reading at or above their grade level. In 1987, the figure was 62.6 per cent. Now East Harlem is in the middle of the performance range for New York's 32 districts.

Chubb and Moe conclude:

> On virtually every relevant dimension, the East Harlem reforms have been a tremendous success. There are lots of schools, emphasising everything from music to science. Teachers are enthusiastic about their work and largely in control of their own schools. They are empowered, professional, and satisfied—all achieved through the natural dynamics of the system, not through the artificiality of bureaucratic rules. School organisations are small and informal, built around team cooperation and coherence of mission. Parents are active, well informed, and take pride in 'their' schools.[10]

The key to success in East Harlem was, not only the empowerment of parents, but also the freeing of the supply side. But the fear of Chubb and Moe—indeed it is a recurring theme of their study—is that the political authorities will reassert their power and end the experiment. It is the political process they fear most. Consequently, their proposals for change urge the de-politicisation of education.

De-Politicisation: The Chubb-Moe Plan for Change

I have devoted considerable space to reviewing Chubb and Moe's account of American educational reform because their study is a significant milestone in the development of our understanding of how best to organise schooling. What makes the study of special importance is their stress, not only on the necessity for the de-politicisation of education policy making but also on the importance of supply-side de-regulation, ironically somewhat neglected by classical liberals.

Based on their assessment of efforts to reform education in the 1970s and 1980s, Chubb and Moe advocate a two-pronged programme of change which combines parent empowerment through vouchers—scholarships in their terminology—with supply-side de-regulation. Consequently, the guiding principle of their plan is that: 'public authority must be put to use in creating a system that is almost entirely beyond the reach of public authority'.[11]

Their scheme is peculiarly relevant to Britain which also has a highly politicised education system which is in the middle of implementing reforms of exactly the type that have already been tried in America. Some of these measures, like the national curriculum, have a centralising effect, others, such as local management of schools and opting out of local authority control to grant-maintained status, involve decentralisation. The centralising measures, such as the national curriculum, tend to suppress competition. The two main decentralising measures, the opting out of schools to grant-maintained status and the local management of schools, show promise, but if Chubb and Moe's analysis of American reforms is correct, these measures will not be enough.

The proposals are also significant because Chubb and Moe offer a role for established providers. School districts (local education authorities here) will no longer enjoy monopoly power but they will have the opportunity to compete and, if successful, to flourish. Chubb and Moe also offer local authorities the opportunity to play a new role as enablers of parental choice instead of monopolists.

A Universal Scholarships Scheme

Chubb and Moe's proposals were made with America in mind, and not every element could fruitfully be shipped over the Atlantic. Narrowed to its bare essentials, their plan may be called a Universal Scholarships Scheme and summarised as follows:

1. The state would define which schools are entitled to receive public funds. The definition should be minimal, covering relatively few matters such as health and safety and minimum standards for teacher certification. The standard should correspond with the criteria for accrediting private schools. The essential point is that the registration of schools under the scheme should not become a significant barrier to the entry of new schools. Teachers, for instance, should not be required to undergo lengthy training. A bachelors degree or its equivalent should be sufficient.

2. Any school that meets the minimum standard must be registered and entitled to receive public funds. Private schools should be included.

3. Every child should be entitled to annual scholarships equivalent to the cost of education. Scholarships could be higher in value for children with special needs, such as the disabled.

4. Parents would have complete choice of school aided by local information centres to provide information and assist choice.

5. Schools would have total control of admissions, school numbers, governing structure, teacher tenure, training and salaries. They would set their own fees and they would not be accountable for their performance to any higher authority, other than parents.

6. Neither the central government nor local authorities would have power over schools. As Chubb and Moe write: 'the very *capacity* for control, not simply its exercise' would be eliminated.[12]

An alternative route for Britain would be to transform all schools into grant maintained schools, thus effectively abolishing local education authorities. This approach might yield considerable benefits, but if Chubb and Moe are right, it would fail sufficiently to de-regulate the supply side. It is now well established that the key to the successful functioning of any market is the possibility that new entrants will take market share from existing schools. Without this discipline, established providers too easily settle down to a cosy co-existence.

To sum up: the traditional case for vouchers has focused on the demand side. Public sector monopolies were to be broken by empowering the consumer through vouchers. It was assumed that this would stimulate competition on the supply side. However, recent American experience suggests that demand-side empowerment cannot alone stimulate competition on the supply side. There must also be radical de-regulation. The ultimate purpose is to re-energise teachers and to re-activate dormant parental responsibility and commitment, and this can only be accomplished if it is possible for new schools to emerge spontaneously to harness the enthusiasm of teachers and parents. Both parent empowerment and supply-side de-regulation are necessary conditions of success.

Notes

1 Levinson, E., *The Alum Rock Voucher Demonstration: Three Years of Implementation*. Santa Monica: Rand Corporation, 1976, P.5631; Rand Corporation, *A Study of Alternatives in American Education*. Santa Monica: Rand Corporation, 1981, R-2170/7-NIE.

2 Raymond J. Domanico, *Model for Choice: A Report on Manhattan's District 4*. New York: Center for Educational Innovation, 1989.

3 *Politics, Markets and America's Schools*. Washington: Brookings Institution, 1990.

4 *Ibid.*, pp. 193-94.

5 *Ibid.*, p. 198.

6 *Ibid.*, p. 201.

7 *Ibid.*, p. 208.

8 *Ibid.*, p. 210.

9 *Ibid.*, pp. 209-11.

10 *Ibid.*, p. 214.

11 *Ibid.*, p. 218.

12 *Ibid.*, p. 226.

2

Educational Services:
Independent Competition or
Maintained Monopoly?

Antony Flew

What Is To Be Done?

The purposes of the present paper are: first, to represent the maintained school system in the UK as what indeed it is—an arrangement for the monopoly supply of primary and secondary educational services to captive consumers; next, progressively to suggest that the ever more widely recognized failures and deficiencies of this system are best understood as being of precisely those kinds most likely to afflict such a state monopoly; and, finally, to inquire whether it is reasonable to hope that the implementation of the 1988 Educational Reform Act will put things right.

So far, so far as I know, there has been very little published discussion of our maintained school system considered as a monopoly. Its monopolistic character is rarely identified as having anything to do with any perceived deficiencies. This diagnostic failure inevitably distorts discussion of projects for improvement.

As so often, both for better and for worse, the USA has here been ahead of the UK. For while their system is perhaps more like, or less unlike, ours than that of any other NATO country, it was back in 1982 that the Pacific Institute for Public Policy Research published R.B. Everhart (Ed.), *The Public School Monopoly* in San Francisco. Since then there have been several other books covering much the same ground and making similar recommendations: for instance, D.T. Kearns and D.P. Doyle, *Winning the Brain Race: A Bold Plan to Make our Schools Competitive*, (San Francisco: Institute for Contemporary Studies, 1988); H.J. Walberg, M.J. Bakalis, J.L. Bast and S. Bauer *We Can Rescue Our Children: The Cure for Chicago's School Crisis*, (Chicago: Heartland Institute, 1988); and, most recently, J.E. Chubb and T.M. Moe, *Politics, Markets and America's Schools*, (Washington: Brookings Institution, 1990).

None of these American works, sustained though they all are by masses of supporting evidence, seems to have received in Britain much attention from what Tom Lehrer once taught its less stuffy participants to call Edbiz. In part no doubt this has to be put down to endemic parochialism. But another part of the explanation must be elsewhere. As Robert Conquest observed over twenty years ago:[1] 'Education is now a vast "interest". An immense lobby attached by conviction, salary and habit, has formed.'

We cannot expect such a lobby to welcome books contending that the sovereign remedy for ills which are consequent upon monopoly in the supply of educational services is: not to continue to pour ever greater resources into the tax-financed maintained system, rewarding apparent failures with further resource inputs; but instead, in one way or another, to introduce competition between individual schools. These, however they may be funded ultimately, should be rewarded immediately for perceived success and penalized for perceived failure.

The National Union of Teachers (NUT) as a major element in that 'interest' is no more ready than its nearest US equivalent, the National Education Association (NEA), to spread the news that Chicago's public schools—described by Secretary of Education William Bennett as 'the worst in the nation'—are not correspondingly underfunded. Per pupil head 'Chicago spends...more than the state and national averages and *three times* the amount spent at parochial schools'.[2] Yet these parochial schools are vastly more successful as educational institutions.[3] The research reported is equally discomfiting to the 'Education ... "interest"':

Higher teacher salaries and smaller class sizes (except class sizes of less than ten) have been found repeatedly to have no significant positive effect on learning. Similarly, total spending per pupil is unrelated to educational results, as are administrators' salaries and teacher experience. In reviewing studies of school district expenditure equalization, ...researchers concluded that increased expenditures go mainly into administrative and auxiliary activities that have little or no effect on educational outcomes.[4]

The Dangers In A State Monopoly

We have for too long failed to attend to Mill's warning. In Chapter V of his classic essay *On Liberty* (1859), and like us here confining his attention to the primary and secondary levels, he picked out as the main dangers of state monopoly in the supply of educational services intellectual indoctrination and Procrustean equalization:

> If the government would make up its mind to *require* for every child a good education, it might save itself the trouble of *providing* one. It might leave to parents to obtain the education where and how they pleased, and content itself with helping to pay the school fees of the poorer classes of children, and defraying the entire school expenses of those who have no one else to pay for them.[5]

But that:

> the whole or any part of the education of the people should be in State hands, I go as far as any one in deprecating.... A general State education is a mere contrivance for moulding people to be exactly like one another: and as the mould in which it casts them is that which pleases the predominant power in the government, whether this be a monarch, a priesthood, an aristocracy, or the majority of the existing generation, in proportion as it is efficient and successful, it establishes a despotism over the mind, leading by natural tendency to one over the body.[6]

Elsewhere and earlier, in *The Principles of Political Economy* (1848), Mill also had something very sharp to say about the economic dangers of monopoly. But he never found occasion to apply any economic ideas of the rational employment of always scarce resources to, in particular, the problems of producing and distributing educational services. No one, however, has ever

18

written more vehemently than Mill against the evils of monopoly, in general. Thus it was that in 1848 he argued, against socialists:

I utterly dissent from the most conspicuous and vehement part of their teaching, their declamations against competition... They forget that wherever competition is not, monopoly is; and that monopoly, in all its forms, is the taxation of the industrious for the support of indolence, if not of plunder... Instead of looking upon competition as the baneful and anti-social principle which it is held to be by the generality of Socialists, I conceive that, even in the present state of society and industry, every restriction of it is an evil, and every extension of it, even if for the time injuriously affecting some class of labourers, is always an ultimate good.[7]

At this point a person whose model for a state monopoly is one of the nationalized industries established by the 1945-50 Labour administration might object to describing the supply of primary and secondary educational services in the UK as such a monopoly. For this system is one in which the maintained schools are owned and, subject to what until quite recently was a comparatively modest amount of central regulation, run by 104 Local Education Authorities (LEAs). The finance supply is supplied, in roughly equal amounts, form both centrally and locally levied taxation.

But these LEAs are more aptly described as Local Education Monopolies (LEMs), since they in fact cater for between 93 per cent and 94 per cent of all the children in relevant cohorts. Certainly that leaves between seven per cent and six per cent attending independent as opposed to maintained schools. So it cannot be denied that this monopoly is still a little less than total. But then, is there any anti-monopoly legislation anywhere in the world which would not be activated long before a single supplier had achieved a 75 per cent or 80 per cent, much less a 93 per cent market share?

All this too is before we take into account a pair of further and weightier considerations. For these LEMs are, both supplying services which it is compulsory to consume, and supplying these free at the point of consumption. So any parents who, after paying the high taxes extorted to finance the state supply of such services, retain sufficient funds to pay the fees charged by independent schools, face a heavily loaded choice. For if they prefer an independent education for their children they have to pay twice: paying once through taxation; and then again by paying private school fees. That any parents at all choose in this sense in these circumstances, and much more that as many as 7 per cent do, should be seen as a damaging indication of at least the perceived nature and quality of the state-supplied product.

The supply free at the point of consumption of services which it is compulsory to accept carries further implications which must concern all of us who will not willingly be led or unresistingly driven *Beyond Freedom and Dignity*.[8] For such arrangements necessarily place all consumers subject to them in the choiceless, subservient and therefore undignified position of beggars. Beggars, notoriously, cannot be choosers. We should recall some never too often quoted words from another document of classical liberalism:

> It is not from the benevolence of the butcher, the brewer or the baker, that we expect our dinner, but from their regard to their own interest.... Nobody but a beggar chuses to depend...upon the benevolence of his fellow citizens. Even a beggar does not depend upon it entirely... The greater part of his occasional wants are supplied in the same manner as those of other people, by treaty, by barter, and by purchase.[9]

Once the maintained system is recognized to be the monopoly which it is, it becomes easy to appreciate the reasons why the entire bureaucratic-educational complex—the teachers' unions, officials in the Department of Education and Science (DES) and in the LEMs, and all other supply side interest groups—are almost unanimously hostile to the voucher or to anything like it. What to some may be more perplexing is the fact that this hostility seems to be shared by most of those professing a peculiar and studiously compassionate concern about the powerlessness of the poor.[10]

It is also worthwhile to note in passing that teachers' unions, which are forever demanding that their members be accorded the status and still more the pay of professionals, consistently neglect to notice that the paying clients of the paradigm professionals —accountants, lawyers, architects, and doctors in private prac- tice—are all, if dissatisfied with the service provided, free to take their business elsewhere. So we may conclude the present section by repeating a denunciation from the Head of a maintained school. It is one altogether typical of spokespersons for the teachers' unions if not, it might be hoped, equally representative of all whom they take it upon themselves to represent:

> We see this as a barrier between us and the parent—this sticky little piece of paper in their hand—coming in and under duress—you will do this or else. We make our judgement because we believe it's in the best of interests of every Willie and every little Johnny... and not because someone's going to say 'if you don't do it, we will do that'. It's this sort of philosophy of the marketplace that we object to.[11]

Indoctrination: Religious And Political

Dangers are not necessarily realized immediately, or even ever. If they were indeed humanly unavoidable, then they would be not dangers but fates. In Britain the beginnings of any sustained and systematic attempt to extend and exploit the state monopoly system as a 'contrivance for moulding people to be exactly like one another'—as an instrument, that is, for the enforcement of the Procrustean ideal—can be dated back only so far as the launching in the late fifties and early sixties of the Comprehensive Revolution.

The teaching of a strictly non-denominational Christianity, however, was by the 1944 Butler Education Act prescribed as the single compulsory element in the syllabi of all maintained schools. Here certainly the original intention was indoctrinative: teaching Religious Knowledge (RK) was to be teaching various favoured religious doctrines as if these were items of knowledge, rather than imparting knowledge of various beliefs in fact held and of practices actually followed.

The period since World War II has, however, been one in which even the ordained leadership of the mainstream churches has become ever more inclined to preach social democratic or socialist politics rather than traditional religion; and to do this while making almost no pretence of having derived these preferred political teachings from any serious or sustained study of the *Bible*.[12] In this period of rising secularization attempts at religious indoctrination in the maintained schools were ever more half-hearted and ever less successful, and the relevant clause in that Act came to be widely treated as a dead letter. A weaker, less effective substitute was ultimately inserted into the 1988 Act.

Whatever may have been done by individual teachers or individual schools, there were until fairly recently no extensive programmes for political indoctrination in the British maintained system. But the last ten or fifteen years have seen an explosion of programmes packed with *suppressiones veri* and *suggestiones falsi*, presupposing legitimately controversial conclusions as their foregone conclusions. Significantly, the main ones being promoted are specifically intended to pervade the entire curriculum.[13] Partly maybe for this reason, and unlike in the religion case, there have here been no provisions for opting out.

For the greater part of the eighties the most widespread kind of political indoctrination was 'Peace Studies'. Since the Soviet threat—or what, by the agents and allies of Soviet imperialism, must have been seen as the promise—has now happily diminished if not altogether disappeared there is, presumably, no longer such a drive to maintain and extend these particular indoctrinative programmes. But at one time they were introduced almost as often as socialists won control of any LEM. Their partisan nature and indoctrinative intent is indicated by the fact that none has ever been found: either to attend at all to the expansionist ambitions and achievements of the USSR; or to reveal the massive superiority of the former Warsaw Pact over NATO in conventional, biological and chemical weaponry.[14]

Suppose now that all the LEMs were to be broken up, and all the schools under their control were in some way to achieve independence. Suppose too that the funds, from whatever public or private pockets they might ultimately be drawn, followed the pupils: so that each individual school stood to gain by attracting and holding pupils and to lose by losing them. Then, absent any relevant regulatory prescription, should we expect the complete elimination of indoctrination? Surely not. For many parents want to have their children indoctrinated into particular sets of favoured beliefs. Yet the fact that other and even the same parents are reluctant to sacrifice teaching time which might otherwise be employed in less controversial ways is bound to constitute one obstacle; while, in a pluralist society, such a free for all would surely ensure that whatever indoctrination there was would at least not be so overwhelmingly one-sided and, as it happens, always left-sided, as it is today.

The Comprehensive Revolution

From the implementation of the 1944 Education Act until the Comprehensive Revolution maintained secondary schools in Britain were almost all of one of two types: on the one hand selective, so-called Grammar Schools, catering for the more academically inclined and gifted; and, on the other hand, non-selective, Secondary Modern Schools, catering for all the rest. At the time when the Act was passed there was talk of a third type, not mentioned in the Act itself, Technical Schools. But, for whatever reasons, very few of these were ever established. Otherwise we might have enjoyed something like the very successful tripartite system of *Gymnasien*, *Realschulen* and *Hauptschulen* introduced in West Germany after 1945.

The revolution consisted in comprehensivization, a.k.a. 'comprehension', the reorganization of the maintained system into nothing but non-selective schools. Such comprehensive neighbourhood schools were to be, in effect, the common schools of John Dewey's educational theory; although references either to Dewey himself or to consequent US experience were, perhaps prudently, eschewed.[15] Since this, like the truly Glorious Revolution of 1688-9, was at least notionally effected through Parliament, we do well to quote from one crucial resolution:

> That this House, conscious of the need to raise educational stan-dards at all levels, and regretting that the realisation of this objective is impeded by the separation of children into different types of secondary schools, notes with approval the efforts of local authorities to reorganise secondary education along comprehensive lines, which will preserve all that is valuable in grammar school education for those children who now receive it and make it available to more

children; ... and believes that the time is now ripe for a declaration
of national policy.

Whatever may be thought of the supporting reasons offered, the
stated aim of this reorganisation was thus entirely and impeccably
educational: namely, to raise the attainment levels of all our
children. No doubt too this has been the actual aim of those who
have run the most educationally successful comprehensive schools.
But equally certainly it has not been the overriding, or even any,
purpose for everyone eager to effect and sustain this revolution.

If only this had indeed been so, then their whole approach would
have been tentative and experimental. They would have been
eager to ensure the monitoring of progress; and ready, if and when
it emerged that levels of strictly educational achievement were not
being raised as predicted, to halt or even to reverse the implementation of the policy.

In fact the contrary has been the case. Not only were no positive
steps taken to ensure that the educational consequences of this
reorganization should be monitored systematically and continuously, but many obstacles were put in the way of anyone wanting to
investigate these consequences. Individual schools and individual
LEMs were permitted to conceal the results achieved in independently assessed examinations, and did. It was only after the school
by school publication of these results had been made compulsory,
by a bitterly contested clause in the 1980 Education Act, that a
systematic and comprehensive study of these results became
possible; although officials at the DES, which had by then been
entirely converted to the ideology of universal compulsory
comprehension,[16] significantly refused to countenance any employment of 'public money' for this crucial heuristic purpose.

The unofficial National Council for Educational Standards
(NCES) therefore rustled up private finance for what was by far
the most exhaustive study ever of such results. Its conclusions,
which the authors themselves chose to print in block capitals, were
that:

SUBSTANTIALLY HIGHER O-LEVEL, CSE AND A-LEVEL
EXAMINATION RESULTS ARE TO BE EXPECTED FOR
PUPILS IN A FULLY SELECTIVE SYSTEM OF SCHOOLS

COMPARED WITH PUPILS IN A FULLY COMPREHENSIVE SYSTEM OF SCHOOLS. THIS FINDING APPLIES TO ALL THE INDICES OF EXAMINATION SUCCESS WHICH WE STUDIED AND, ACCORDING TO OUR DATA, IS AS ROBUST AS THE GENERALLY ACCEPTED FINDING THAT EXAMINATION RESULTS ARE HIGHLY CORRELATED WITH SOCIAL CLASS.[17]

'Labour's Equality Machine'

Upon the publication of these findings the researchers were subject to a sustained and scurrilous campaign of vilification. Both their methods and their findings were contemptuously dismissed, on the grounds that these, in a document which as unofficial outsiders they themselves were not permitted to see, had been 'rubbished' by the professional statisticians of the DES. Although the researchers eventually got a sight of that document, and although the DES statisticians in a consequent face to face discussion admitted—very honestly and creditably—that the mistake had been theirs, and although the NCES findings were later substantially confirmed by the DES itself, the vilifiers were largely successful in concealing from any wider public the rubbishing of the rubbishers.[18]

The immediate relevance to us of all this lies in the fact that apparently none of the most vociferous vilifiers has ever allowed the discovery that those findings are as robust as could reasonably be expected in any way to affect their own commitment to maintaining and extending the Comprehensive Revolution. This shows that, whatever the original motivation of these people, it cannot now be, simply and straightforwardly, that of the Parliamentary resolution. For many union barons and professional politicians it is presumably a matter of a bigoted and stubborn refusal to admit that a policy of their party is not producing the results promised. But there have certainly been others for whom from the beginning the main purpose was frankly Procrustean rather than purely educational.

Professor A.H. Halsey, for instance, played an important part both in campaigning for a universal compulsory comprehensive system and in directing or—some would say—misdirecting supposedly relevant research into all sorts of inequalities. Later in the year of that resolution he wrote in *New Society* (17 June 1965), under the title 'Education and Equality': 'Some people, and I am one, want to use education as an instrument in pursuit of an egalitarian society.'

Indeed they do! Many of them, for instance, have insisted that to be truly comprehensive schools must eschew streaming or setting, and practice mixed ability teaching at all times and in all subjects. So much for the promise, of which so much used to be made in pro-comprehensive propaganda, that a child's whole educational future should not depend on the results of one examination at age 11+, but that it should be possible and easy to move pupils up or down within a single institution throughout the whole period of their secondary schooling. For now, if these people have their way everywhere, there will never again be any fast or slow lanes for anybody.

That the ending of all streaming and setting, and the institution of mixed ability teaching at all times and in all subjects, are essential elements in the comprehensive idea was suggested by, for instance, many contributors to series still much recommended in institutions for teacher training. Thus, in an article under the menacing title 'The Comprehensive School: Labour's Equality Machine', Dennis Marsden reassures himself: 'that the narrowly meritocratic emphasis on streaming and academic results... will be a temporary phase', since 'the internal dynamic of reorganisation should begin to assert itself'; and that 'These early disappointments for egalitarians emphasise that the community and the meritocratic schools represent quite different ideals... meritocrats and egalitarians will want to evaluate education, even the 'development of talent', by different criteria'.[19]

Again, and ten years later, another extremely influential professional educationist faulted many actually existing schools for defecting from the comprehensive ideal; in as much as 'what can fairly be called the grammar-school curriculum continued to hold its central and dominating position... despite comprehensive reorganization'.[20] Recognizing that children differ, and hence that such a curriculum is not suitable for everyone, he nevertheless insisted, in the name of that ideal, that all children must follow the same curriculum, albeit one designed with the majority in mind—a 'central core curriculum...organized around community studies and the expressive arts'.[21] This, as this distinguished educationist is not ashamed to add, will remove the 'cognitive—intellectual' element from the education of all our children!

Another item in what is widely seen as the ultimate, anti-meritocratic, egalitarian-collectivist logic of comprehension is the demand for a single, unified and undivisive examination system; a system designed to cater for the entire ability range. Thus, in a pamphlet *Examining at 16+: The Case for a Common System*, issued in November, 1978, the NUT proclaimed, without apparent hesitation or embarrassment, that 'In maintaining two quite separate examinations, designed for pupils of different ability ranges, the present system is as divisive, and hence educationally indefensible, as the co-existence of grammar and secondary modern schools' (p.2). For the same reason they went on to argue that in their own ideal, all-in, non-arbitrary, egalitarian world, 'there would be no artificial division between "pass" and "fail"' (p. 6).[22] Yet how is any education at all to proceed, if it is thus impermissibly inegalitarian and divisive to distinguish between success and failure in teaching and learning?

Although it is impossible to be certain how far breaking up the Local Education Monopolies and exposing the newly liberated schools to the incentives and disciplines of a competitive market would diminish the total and alter the direction of indoctrinative activity, it is quite obvious that such measures must preempt the project of using 'education as an instrument' for imposing the Procrustean ideal of equality of outcome upon the recalcitrant diversity of individual talents, temperaments and inclinations. For what parents, given the choice, would not prefer a school which treated their children as the different individuals which they are to one concerned to make them more alike?[23] It is indeed precisely because it constitutes the only instrument with which Procrustean social engineers can reasonably hope to equalize that recalcitrant diversity—those to them intolerably divisive inequalities—that a total, all-comprehensive state monopoly is so intensely and so urgently desired.

Deficient Measures of Performance

It is most remarkable—yet still more remarkable that it should so rarely be noticed, and protested as a scandal—that in this huge monopoly industry, which is by any criterion one of the largest in the country, there is no comprehensive system for assessing performance; no comprehensive system, that is, for measuring educational value added (EVA). The independently assessed national examinations—GCE and CSE, and their significantly less independently assessed successor GCSE, were specifically designed to cater only for the top 60 per cent of the whole ability range. No school-leaving examinations have ever been similarly directed at the bottom 40 per cent. So we find that up to half of all those who choose to drop out of the system at the first legal opportunity leave without any credible certification showing how much, if at all, they may have benefited from all their years of compulsory education.

This failure or, perhaps better, this refusal to produce the evidence which would be yielded by independently assessed school-leaving examinations for the bottom 40 per cent is scandalous in two ways. First, because it constitutes a failure to provide the leavers themselves with reliable evidence of their educational achievement, and consequent employability. Second, because it constitutes a failure or, in this case more surely, a refusal to provide the taxpaying public with similarly reliable evidence of the actual performance of a nationalized industry into which we taxpayers continue to pour ever-increasing resources.[24]

One significant, yet once again, rarely remarked consequence of this failure or refusal to provide evidence of performance at the lowest level is that whenever committees are established to report on and make recommendations about levels of literacy or numeracy these have to begin by somehow constructing their own more or less conjectural estimates of the extent of the problem. If only adequate and comprehensive tests were being given within the system itself, then such inquiries could start from the firm and precise findings of these tests. But in that case, of course, if gross and extensive deficiencies in basic educational achievement had been revealed, then these revelations themselves might well have been sufficient to generate powerful and promptly effective pressures to improve the abysmal performance of the state education monopoly.

Studies by the Institute of Mathematics and later for the National Institute of Economic and Social Research (NIESR) should have been, but were not, sufficient to shake the complacencies of the bureaucratic-educational establishment.[25] The former found, for instance, that a quarter of the sixteen year olds in the schools of the Inner London Education Authority (ILEA) —the authority, by the way, which was then spending about 40 per cent per pupil head above average—could not do calculations as simple as 6 x 79, even given pencil and paper.

The same inquiry incidentally yielded something important which had not been sought—an initial indication of the extent of post-registration truancy (PRT). Although this phenomenon must concern anyone sincerely committed to truly universal education, nevertheless for many years it proved impossible to interest the DES in sponsoring further research. Only very recently, and some months after the completion and the publication of the findings of a private study severely limited by lack of resources,[26] was the DES finally persuaded to support and finance a far more extensive inquiry.

The NIESR investigation compared the standards achieved at various levels of ability in West Germany and in England. It found that at the top of the ability range these were roughly comparable, whereas:

> Attainment...*by those in the lower half of the ability range in England appeared to lag by the equivalent of about two years' schooling behind the corresponding section of pupils in Germany* (emphasis original).

For literacy the indices have until very recently been more indirect. Thus in *The Times* for 22 July 1983, under the headline 'At least 2 million illiterate adults in Britain, report says', the Education Correspondent wrote of a sample survey—in which the Basic Skills

Unit had not actually tested adults but simply asked whether they felt themselves to be handicapped by illiteracy—that the resulting estimate 'confirms earlier figures which were based on guesswork'. Yet, neither she nor, it seemed, any other commentator went on to deplore the lack of direct and comprehensive data from the schools. Nor yet to point out that, if the system had really been committed to ensuring that no one left school either illiterate or innumerate, then, as an indispensable part of the teaching process proper, tests would have been given; and that, by merely collecting and publishing the results of these tests, all guesstimates could have been replaced by knowledge.

'Independently assessed' is a crucial qualification here. 'Pupil profiles' constructed by the pupils' own teachers are not to be relied on save in so far as they can be and are cross-checked against the findings of independently assessed public examinations. For, necessarily, such examinations test at one and the same time: both the pupils' learning, and the content and effectiveness of the teachers' teaching. Partly for this obvious reason of self-interest, but partly too from a generous inclination to think too well of those whom we have ourselves been teaching, we are all inclined to over-estimate the educational achievements of our own pupils.

This often unrecognized yet inescapable ambiguity in findings from examinations of taught work makes appeals to abandon independent assessment, appeals which are too often made either by or on behalf of teachers, outrageous and altogether unacceptable. For any such call is a call to abandon a fundamental principle of natural justice—that no one should be judge in their own cause. A further dimension of unreliability is introduced when the pupil work to be assessed is course work—work, that is, not done under examination conditions. For by giving weight to this we both supply incentive to cheat and jettison the previous guarantee that what is being assessed is the unaided work of the pupil.

Invalidating Direct Year-on-year Comparisons

That existing measures of performance do not embrace all pupils passing through the system is not, however, by any means their only major deficiency. For GCE, CSE and presumably now also

GCSE examinations were not designed to reveal whether performance is improving from year to year. On the contrary: in 1960 the sometime Secondary Schools Examinations Council (SSEC) recommended that in future all such examinations should be norm-related rather than criteria-related.[27] (In the former case the examiners aim to award the same grades to roughly the same proportions of all candidates presenting at the same time, in the latter they attempt the more exacting task of ensuring that given levels of attainment always get the same grading.) In so far as this SSEC recommendation is followed—and later, in 1964, the newly formed Schools Council was to endorse it emphatically—the resulting practice must necessarily invalidate all direct year-on-year comparisons.

Even where proper measurements of performance have been made there is always strong resistance to publicizing these in any form making even same year comparative judgements possible, whether these be of educational effectiveness or of economic efficiency in the employment of resources. Thus the National Union of Teachers (NUT), the largest of all the British teachers' unions, declared its 'total opposition' to the clause in the 1980 Education Bill requiring all maintained schools to publish the results achieved by their pupils in public examinations. For, said the NUT, the results so published would often be misinterpreted, and their publication would lead to the construction of 'league tables'.

There never was, of course, any proposal to prevent schools adding whatever further information they thought to be necessary in order to put their achievements or their lack of achievements into correct perspective—information, that is, about the social mix of successive intakes, about peculiar local difficulties, and so on. With regard to the continuing commitment of the NUT to the suppression of all data making comparisons and consequent competition possible, we may most aptly quote shrewd words from the masterpiece of England's most formidable political thinker: 'It is easy to see the benefit of such darkness, and to whom it accrueth.'[28]

The resolve of monopolists to suppress information about performance, and their relative lack of concern to remedy their own demonstrated deficiencies, is most clearly visible in the matter of basic literacy. For many years individual parents and other interested persons have been complaining about failures or refusals to teach children to read. They have had precious little success in their efforts: either to extract information from particular LEMs; or to secure improvements. Until very recently all that had emerged fairly definitely was that there is a general tendency to impose the doctrines and preferred practices of a 'progressive-egalitarian' ideology. This has for years been propagated in most of our teacher training institutions, and is now dominant through-out the entire bureaucratic-educational complex. In defiance of abundant research evidence showing that the traditional method of beginning by picking out letters to make words—C-A-T spells cat ('phonics')—is for most children the most effective, progres-sive-egalitarianism condemns such didactic teaching (i.e. teaching) as merely instilling 'decoding skills' (i.e. teaching to read).

In 1989 there was a break-through or, better, a break-out. Educational psychologists from ten LEMs—only one of whom dared to reveal his name or, consequently, the identity of his employers—pooled and published the previously top secret results of reading tests given and taken over many years.[29] The average reported *decline* from 1985 to 1989 is over three points of a standard score, implying a 50 per cent rise in the proportion of very poor readers. This decline shows over a range of tests. Over five years more than a quarter of a million pupils were tested, equivalent each year to nearly 10 per cent of all seven-year olds in the UK.

For us the prime significance of this affair is: that these LEMs were resolved to suppress information which, it is obvious, was of great public and particularly parental concern; and that they threatened to discipline any of their employees who dared conscientiously to break the silence. Apparently too, none of them saw this substantial decline in performance, revealed to them and to them only by their own secret tests, as a sufficient reason to challenge recently adopted and recommended but demonstrably ineffective teaching methods. The political masters of these LEMs are of all political colours, yet all are thus it seems united both in their concern to conceal the evidence of decline and in their lack of concern to take steps to reverse it.

Note too that all this evidence of educational ineffectiveness also points to economic inefficiency. For the sharp increase in very poor readers resulting from non-didactic teaching (i.e. not teaching) is then seen as demanding and justifying the appointment of more remedial teachers and—because poor readers often become 'statemented' 'special needs' cases—more teachers' aids. If only all individual schools were subject to economic pressures to perform effectively, it would become scarcely possible to maintain such preposterous and perverse inefficiencies.

The Input/Output Equation

It is, as was insisted in the two previous sections, most remarkable —yet still more remarkable that it should so rarely be noticed, and protested as a scandal—that in this huge monopoly education industry there is no comprehensive system for assessing performance, for measuring EVA. It is a second equally remarkable fact, and one equally rarely remarked and protested, that it appears to be almost universally assumed that in this particular and peculiar industry every increase or any reduction in resource input must—at least as nearly as may in an incorrigibly imperfect world reasonably be demanded—guarantee a corresponding increase or reduction in education output (EVA). These two facts are surely related, the second as a part cause and presumably also a part consequence of the first.

It is not of course surprising that such an assumption is made by spokespersons for the teachers' unions and other supply side interest groups. It was, for instance, made in leaflets issued in 1979-80 by the NUT as part of what was called a 'Campaign against the Cuts'—notwithstanding that these were not actual reductions in spending but only in previously projected increases. In fury the NUT told the world: that 'government policy means... less education for your child'; and that 'Scrooge lived to regret his meanness'. It called for 'protest about the threat to education standards'.

Yet the only standards over which they themselves appeared in fact to be aroused, and to which what evidence they did produce actually was directed, were not educational at all. They were not, that is to say, standards achieved in and by teaching and learning. Instead they were all a matter of how many people were being or were to be employed as teachers; of how much tax money was to be spent on school meals; and generally, of the total public expenditure falling under the sometimes misleading budgetary heading 'Education'. Much the same criticism applies to the advertisements issued by the NUT eleven years later, although now the call for higher pay for teachers was perhaps even louder than before.

What should, however, be more surprising is to find that same extraordinary identification of resource input with education output made by an outstandingly able man, who had previously served both as Economics Fellow of Trinity College, Oxford and the Minister of State at the DES. Under the administration of which he had been a member, he wrote: 'expenditure on education rose from 4.8 per cent of GNP in 1964 to 6.1 per cent. As a result, all classes of the community enjoyed significantly more education than before'.[30] The second of these propositions was thus presumably asserted as an immediate inference from the first. For the only further statement which might perhaps have been construed as a premise is: 'The huge expansion in the supply of teachers produced a steady reduction in the pupil/teacher ratio'.

In truth there are most excellent reasons both theoretical and practical for challenging this misguiding identification. As a sometime professional economist the writer ought, even more than the rest of us, to have recognized that monopoly suppliers, not subject to any of the salutary disciplines of competition, are scarcely likely to provide equally good and always the best possible value for money to all their captive clients. By contrast no firm can hope to survive very long in a market if it persists in charging much more and/or in offering a much inferior product than is being charged or offered by the competition.

Since the UK lacks a suitable battery of criteria-related examin-ations, we cannot consult their findings in order to settle the practical question whether rising resource input has in fact been rewarded by a corresponding rise in educational output. But the USA has misleadingly named Scholastic Aptitude Tests (SAT), taken by everyone hoping to proceed to higher education. These SATs are criteria-related, and in fact assess performance rather than aptitude. 1965, the year of the passing of the Elementary and Secondary Education Act, marked the beginnings of series: both of massive annual *increases* in the overall funding of the public schools; and of significant annual *declines* in the average SAT scores—declines which were checked first only in the early eighties and which have not even yet been decisively reversed.[31]

Such evidence should be sufficient to establish: not, of course, that in such systems resource input and education output correlate negatively; but only—and what is surely more than sufficient—that the common assumption of a direct proportionality between resource input and education output is preposterous.

'Improving' The Ratios?

Something specific also needs to be said about the most important particular case under the general assumption that in education resource input equals output. In any other industry we should expect economists to construe what are here called *improvements* in the pupil/teacher ratio as at least prima facie evidence of overpersonning. But the NUT began the first of its recent series of advertisements: 'Educationists say that there should be no more than 25 children in a school class. Any more and a child's ability to learn begins to suffer. In Britain today there are often over 40 in a class.'

Certainly this is the sort of thing which educationists in the UK and the USA do say; and politicians; and Uncle Tom Cobleigh and all. But this more particular assumption is one for which adequate support is rarely asked and never offered. Once the crucial question is put, and pressed, it emerges that no one can point to hard evidence showing that, within the relevant range—say from

45 to 15—reductions in class size tend to make teaching more effective, as opposed to more agreeable. If anything the available research findings point in the opposite direction. And in Japan, where performance is far superior across all subjects in which cross-cultural comparisons can be and have been made, 'teachers typically teach large classes of 40 or even 50 children'.[32]

Even if we did know that all reductions within the relevant ranges do make for more and/or better pupil learning, across all subjects and at all levels, still anyone sincerely and rationally dedicated to obtaining the best possible educational results from whatever resources may from time to time become available would nevertheless want to press the question with which the poet Yeats is said to have responded to the news of his Nobel Prize for Literature: 'How much? How Much?'

For with scarce resources—and resources, especially money, are always scarce—there are always opportunity costs to consider; namely, all the alternatives which have to be forgone if it is decided to devote those resources to one particular purpose rather than another. Remember too that, because so large a proportion of all education budgets goes on teachers' salaries, what may be a practically insignificant 'improvement' in overall ratios has to be bought at the cost of forgoing a relatively massive expansion of, for instance, school libraries.

Two further often overlooked considerations need to be mentioned. First: even if it were to be established as a general law that, all other things being equal, smaller classes always make for more effective teaching, nevertheless it very rarely is the case that all other things actually are equal. Thus the more teachers recruited—again all other things being equal—the lower will be the average quality and qualifications of those teachers. In 1975/6, for instance, during a great drive to 'improve' the ratios, 'Of all the students accepted for training, 41 per cent had not been able to pass O-level mathematics'.[33] Second: teachers appear curiously unaware that the lower the pupil/teacher ratio the more difficult it becomes to fund generous salary increases. It is therefore obviously in their interests, though not so obviously in the interests of the officials of their unions, to keep the profession as small as possible.

Suppose, however—as, in default of further and more decisive evidence we surely must—that 'improvements' in pupil/teacher ratios make classroom activities more agreeable for the teachers and/or for the pupils rather than that they make for significant improvements in learning. Then it certainly does not follow that it must be irrational to continue making reductions in these ratios; instead of halting the whole process, or even putting it into reverse. What actually would be irrational would be to continue the necessary expenditures without meeting the consequent need for a fresh justification.

For, if and in so far as the aim is no longer to improve the learning of pupils but instead to increase the job satisfaction of their teachers, then spending for this purpose should be taken into account in all salary negotiations with the teachers' unions. Alternatively or additionally, if and in so far as the aim is to make the classroom experience more agreeable to pupils, then the question arises of what the pupils and their parents would have to say about the opportunity costs of this particular employment of the relevant resources.

Actually Declining Productivity

Presumably it was despair, both over the inadequacy of the available measures of education outputs and about the consequent almost complete lack of economic rationality in the allocation of resource inputs, which led the author of what is still the standard introduction to the economics of education to devote only one of his ten chapters to 'The Microeconomics of Education'.[34] This chapter comprises three sections: 'Efficiency for what?'; 'The productivity of educational systems'; and 'The advent of programme budgeting in education'. Using those indisputably inadequate measures of outputs, which were nevertheless all that the monopoly system itself saw fit to provide, the author calculated his way to what should have been the shattering conclusion:

> that the productivity of secondary education fell drastically between 1950 and 1963, irrespective of the view we take of the goals of

secondary education; in fact, productivity declined at an annual rate of at least 2 per cent a year over the thirteen year period.[35]

And that:

Unless the quality of those who left school in this period has increased in a way that no one has yet been able to measure, or unless there are aims of education in terms of which output may be said to have risen significantly although no one has yet been able to quantify these aims, we may conclude that it took more resources to produce a standard secondary-school leaver in 1963 than in 1950.[36]

From the top down the reaction of almost everyone in Edbiz, if such conclusions can somehow be forced on their attention, is to tell us that they do not really believe in examinations or, rather better, that examinations are not everything. From this latter and entirely uncontentious premise it is then customary to conclude, as an immediate inference, that they are not anything. At the time when this author must have been writing, and calculating, the Minister in charge of the DES—Edward Short, an ex-Headmaster of a maintained school and himself married to a Headmistress —'condemned examinations as a great disincentive to true education, hanging like a millstone around the necks of the schools'.[37]

Now it is all very well, and entirely correct, to insist that there certainly are some desirable kinds of learning achievement which are not adequately assessable by means of two or three hour written examinations. For instance: the success or failure of an exercise in moral education—something largely and perhaps grievously neglected since it has been assumed to be compassed within the itself increasingly neglected activity of Religious Instruction (RI)—is surely not to be determined by references to the pupils' ability to regurgitate moral maxims. More relevant would be before and after indices: both of theft and bullying within the school; and of the grosser forms of delinquency outside.[38] But to undertake to teach somebody something, when you cannot propose any means of determining whether or not you have succeeded, is about as sensible as, albeit far less entertaining than, *The Hunting of the Snark*.

Such irrational contempt for every kind of testing has to be seen as symptomatic of a radical insincerity of educational purpose. Descartes once remarked that, in determining what people sincerely believed, he preferred to look to what they did rather than to what they said. His advice is equally sound with regard to sincerity in general. Hence, in order to prove that they are indeed sincerely pursuing some purpose, the one thing above all which people have to do is constantly to monitor their success or failure in fulfilling that purpose. If ever and whenever this monitoring reveals that they are not succeeding, all truly sincere purposers will there and then make that sincerity plain by their eagerness to seek and their readiness to adopt fresh tactics apparently offering better promise of success.

Economic As Educational Efficiency

That brief and elementary philosophical excursus carries important, indeed explosive, practical implications. For if once we have learned to appreciate the logically necessary connections between sincerity of purpose, rationality and the monitoring of success or failure in achieving whatever purposes are being sincerely pursued, then we can scarcely fail to raise and to press upsetting questions about the activities and inactivities of the entire bureaucratic-educational complex.

In this perspective it becomes quite clear that it will not do for professing educators superciliously to dismiss as irrelevant and banausic questions about the economically efficient deployment of whatever resources may from time to time be available to them. On the contrary: precisely to the extent that they are indeed single mindedly committed to achieving the maximum output of whatever they conceive to be the educational goods, they must become concerned to discover the particular deployment of those resources which will indeed yield the maximum of those goods; which is to say, by definition, the economically most efficient deployment.

It was a decade ago when various writers for the then newly established Social Affairs Unit (SAU) began to argue that the welfare state—by which was meant all the tax funded organizations for the supply of health, education, and welfare services—

'*distributes the burden of proof unfairly... It is the welfare state that consumes public money and it is its obligation to prove that it is not wasting it...* Since it is the welfare state that has the resources for assessment, it is up to it to use them.'[39]

That intellectually compelling argument, frequently repeated in subsequent publications, nevertheless appears to have made precious little impact upon those who person these organizations. (Externally, however, it has led to the establishment of the Audit Commission, which has for instance drawn public attention to the enormous waste involved in maintaining redundant school places.) The SAU argument can now be reinforced by a challenge pressing closer to the bone. For it is not only that these Welfare State organizations are better placed to assess their own efficiency in employing available resources than are any outside critics. More importantly, this is something which they must constantly be doing if they really are sincerely and straightforwardly committed, within the limits of the resource input available to them, to maximizing their output of whatever services they are supposed to be supplying.

Union officials, along with their friends in Parliament and in the media, are forever calling for still more spending; and are always very ready to denounce Ministerial opposition as deriving from a heartless and miserly indifference to the needs of those to whom state supplied health, education and welfare services are rendered.[40] But unless these querulous compassionists demand that welfare state organizations continuously assess their own operations, and demonstrate that they are not wasting tax moneys, the charge of indifference about the actual provision of services ought to, but almost never does, rebound upon its makers.

Confining ourselves here to the case of education, we have of course to insist first that any adequate assessment of the efficiency of the maintained school monopoly is impossible without a fully comprehensive system of independent, criteria-related tests and examinations of pupil performance. Absent this essential we will nevertheless notice here two gross inefficiencies about which impressive evidence has emerged.

(i) Because even at the beginning of the Comprehensive Revolution people able and willing to teach mathematics, the hard sciences and foreign languages up to A-level were already a scarce resource it was foreseeable, and in fact by many foreseen, that that reorganization, so far from offering 'a grammar school education for all', would in fact deprive many able working class boys and girls of the grammar school education which otherwise they would have enjoyed.[41] At a time when LEMs were still permitted to conceal such matters of public concern the A-level results from 90 of the then rather more than 180 always comprehensive schools run by ILEA fell into the hands of two extremely energetic NCES researchers. (Perhaps, as the phrase goes, these secret results 'fell off the back of a lorry'?) Strongly protesting that to publish these alone would be misleading, ILEA's Director of Education nevertheless refused to release the rest. So the researchers proceeded to publish an analysis of all they had.[42]

To anyone sincerely concerned for the education, as opposed to the equalization, of all our children, as those researchers were, and are, the results were appalling. Of those 90 ILEA comprehensive schools, 36 had no A-level French or Geography, 28 no Physics, 25 no Chemistry, 22 no Mathematics and 20 no Biology. Just how wastefully the available teachers were employed is seen from the further fact that 46.5 per cent of the subject groups in eight major subjects produced no more than two A-level entries; and, hence, even fewer passes. These and other figures given in that NCES report point to two important conclusions. First, and certainly, that some very precious teachers were being very wastefully employed to teach very tiny classes. Second, and somewhat less certainly, that a lot of able and willing children were confined in schools unable to provide A-level teaching from which they could have benefited, and which was available elsewhere under the same LEM.

(ii) A second index of massive waste is the disparity between expenditure in and on the maintained schools themselves ('at the chalkface') and expenditure on external administrators, inspectors and advisers—whether these are people based at the DES or people working in and out of Town and Shire Halls. To provide ideally appropriate standards of comparison we need research into the finances of the surviving independent day schools. For certainly, before the introduction of GCSE, these schools contrived to produce an utterly disproportionate number of all O- and A-level passes with, it would seem, next to no similarly 'external' expenditures.[43]

But in default of such directly relevant comparative findings we may best turn to a report published in the *Daily Mail* for 13 November 1990. It appears that there are now nearly 400,000 non-teachers employed by the DES and the LEMs. Of this total, which is just about equal to the total of teachers employed in the classrooms, up to one-third are engaged in educational administration. During the preceding year, while the number of classroom teachers dropped by over 5,000, the number of non-teachers went up by 2,500. Even more significantly, during the previous ten years the number of teachers employed by LEMs but not employed to teach children increased from 3.7 per cent to 7.7 per cent of the total teaching force. David Hart, of the Association of Head Teachers, estimates that there are nearly 20,000 educational advisers in the LEMs, at a total annual cost of nearly half a billion pounds.[44]

Figures such as these can do much to explain why it is that many of those who have been serving at the chalk face firmly believe that there have since 1979 been savage cuts, notwithstanding that overall spending under the budget rubric 'Education' has during the years increased, *in real terms*, by over 40 per cent per pupil head.[45] For the truth is that in many LEMs and in many of their schools, there have in fact been hurtful economies 'at the chalk face'—hurtful economies making room for extravagances elsewhere. Another form of such extravagant waste must be mentioned. This is the maintaining of huge numbers of redundant school places. The Audit Commission recently estimated that this is costing a cool £800 million a year.[46]

The widespread, stubbornly persistent belief that the maintained school system is grossly underfunded and has been suffering savage cuts—a popular misconception devotedly fostered by all the supply side interest groups and their political creatures—seems all too likely to ensure that future administrations will continue the tradition of constantly increasing overall funding without ever pressing upon the entrenched bureaucratic-educational establishment penetrating enquiries about the educational effectiveness of alternative resource allocations. Yet, as we have surely shown, these are a kind of hard questions which ought to have been, and to be, being asked and answered all the time.

People arguing for ever greater spending on the National Health Service often point to the example of other major EEC countries, such as France and Germany, which devote larger proportions of their larger Gross National Product (GNP) to health services. Whatever the value of such an argument in that context, the parallel argument here is worthless. For the UK already spends a *higher* proportion of GNP on the supply of educational services than either Germany or Japan. Yet wherever cross-cultural comparisons are possible, and have been made, their standards of achievement are much better.[47] By contrast the USA, which regularly outspends other countries, fails ruinously in such international comparisons.[48]

So once again we have to reiterate morals which almost anywhere else would scarcely need to be asserted at all. These are: not only that it is not how much you spend that matters, but how effectively you spend it; but also that you cannot hope to spend effectively, and in an economically rational way, until and unless you have equipped yourself with comprehensive and reliable measures of the effects actually effected.[49]

Will The 1988 Act Set Things Right?

Within that most important 1988 Act there are two conflicting tendencies. The dominant tendency is *dirigiste*, centralizing, homogenizing and bureaucratic. Few, if any, Acts of the Mother of Parliaments can ever have granted more fresh powers of direction to Ministers. Under this Act—which I have heard one Junior Minister at the DES describe beneath his breath as the Education Nationalization Act—all maintained schools are required to devote almost all of what one must now ruefully recognise as often their class rather than their teaching time to a uniform National Curriculum. It is now not for the schools, or for the LEMs, but for the Minister to decide for which public examinations they are to be permitted to prepare and enter pupils. An so on. And on and on and on. The other, opposite, far and away weaker tendency in the 1988 Act is towards decentralization, and giving parents more influence upon, and more room for choice between, alternative providers of educational services for their children.

(1) That weaker, decentralizing tendency, with its promise of demonopolization and consequent improvement through competition, has to a considerable extent been neutralized and frustrated by the intrusions of the dominant directive and centralizing drive towards a more intensive and uniform monopolistic provision. This is by no means inherent in the nature of regulation as such. For just as monopoly positions, though in fact frequently abused, nevertheless do not necessarily and inevitably have to be abused, so central regulation does not have to be, nor is it in fact always and everywhere, either Procrustean or otherwise misguided.

In the present case the main source of trouble has been successive Ministers allowing the crucial committees, commissions and working parties charged with the detailed practical implementation of the Act to be dominated by the same sort of people, and sometimes the very same people, as have been responsible for reducing our maintained school system to the catastrophic condition which that 1988 Act was supposed to remedy.[50] These 'progressive egalitarians'[51] remain more or less openly resolved to frustrate the reforming purposes of that 1988 Act.[52] It is significant that among the original appointees to the National Curriculum Council (NCC) and the Schools Examinations and Assessment Council (SEAC) there was not even one person who had been prominent among the longtime critics calling for radical reform of the previous establishment.

Certainly it is difficult to believe, if once all existing maintained schools were to be deprived of their present monopoly privileges, and thus became competing individual firms subject to the incentives and disciplines of the market, that reliable measures of the teaching effectiveness at all levels of those schools would not—absent restrictive regulation—be rapidly evolved and publicized. For everybody knows that firms competing to sell their products strive to demonstrate the quality of those products to possible purchasers. However, the fewer and the less reliable the measures available when this reform was initiated, then the greater and the more protracted the teething troubles to be expected.

Reformers are understandably impatient to put an end to the scandal of allowing a substantial but apparently unknown proportion of those escaping school at the first legal opportunity to go out without any reliable certification of what, if anything, they have succeeded in mastering—during their ten years of compulsory education.[53] Such reformers might not unreasonably call for the immediate imposition by central regulation of some sort of national minimum curriculum, leading to a certification of minimal employability and minimal fitness for citizenship.

Assuming, however, that those understandably impatient reformers were committed to the generous ideal erected in the Parliamentary resolution quoted in Section 4, above—the ideal of ensuring that all our children reach the different highest educational levels of which they are severally capable—then for them this minimum would be no more than a most elementary and basic core to which the more talented pupils would need to devote only a small and progressively diminishing proportion of their class time. But a National Curriculum which is to take always and in every successive year of compulsory schooling the greater part of everyone's class time is a curriculum crafted to satisfy the cravings of Procrusteans—people dedicated to the meanly repressive ideal of ensuring that all should reach and none exceed a universal, uniform, and hence supposedly undivisive mediocrity.

About the actual content of the British National Curriculum as so far revealed there is little which it is either possible or appropriate to say here. It is not possible to say much because it has been in operation for only one pupil year, and that the first year of the 1990-91 entry. And here it is appropriate to refer only to what is most directly consequent upon the monopoly status of the maintained system. But it is clear that, if the NCC as at present structured continues to get its way, then some of Mill's perhaps exaggerated fears of 'a mere contrivance for moulding people to be exactly like one another' will indeed be realized. For the NCC apparently plans to fill almost all the class time of all pupils with the same materials, while the selection of items for inclusion in this uniform and mandatory pabulum seems to be being determined largely in terms of conventional 'progressive-egalitarian' values and beliefs.[54]

As for SEAC, it is here both necessary and sufficient to insist that it has shown no awareness whatsoever of the imperative need for independent and objective testing, conducted under examination conditions. Had SEAC been given a clear mandate to construct tests to meet that need for the seven year olds who constitute the one cohort which has yet been tested, and had it been disposed straightforwardly to fulfil such a mandate, then it surely could and would have produced a suitably serviceable series of pencil and paper tests, to be performed under properly strict examination conditions, and consuming at most three or four periods on successive days. Instead SEAC developed an excruciatingly elaborate exercise for eliciting from teachers innumerable highly subjective judgements on pupils whom they had themselves been teaching and of performances put up under informal and uncontrolled conditions.[55] This preposterous programme was scheduled to consume up to three weeks of what might otherwise have served as valuable teaching time.

(ii) The opposite and weaker tendency in the 1988 Act is, as was said earlier, 'towards decentralization and giving parents more influence upon, and more room for choice between, alternative providers of educational services for their children'. We may distinguish three sorts of moves in this opposite, centrifugal direction. The first and least important are those giving parents slightly more influence in determining which of the schools maintained by the local LEM their own children are to attend. The second sort is of those resulting in what is called the Local Management of Schools or—to the confusion of those able to remember British railways before nationalization—LMS. The third sort is of provisions for opting out of the control of the local LEM

and becoming—in Margaret Thatcher's oxymoronic phrase—
'independent state schools'.

To all friends of individual freedom and individual choice any
and every liberalizing move, however, small must be welcome.
Nevertheless it is important to emphasize just how small and how
inadequate these first sort of moves are. At best they provide more
voice rather than more exit. But, notoriously, more voice means in
practice mainly more voice for those who are already articulate,
pushing and persistent. Nor is there much reason to expect that
these particular moves will—unlike their equally well-intentioned
predecessors—very substantially diminish the power and inclination
of officials to say 'No!'

People occupying official positions within the bureaucratic-
educational complex are not only to a large extent able to control
the supply of relevant information. They also have the lion's share
in determining how many places are assumed to be available in
which institutions. For this is as much a matter of legal
prescription as of objective fact: if the authorities really want to
squeeze a few more in, then this is almost always possible. And
whenever officials have their own reasons for wanting to fill and
to keep full schools which parents perceive as unsuitable and
unsatisfactory for their children, then the officials can, and will,
refer smugly to their statutory responsibility to ensure the
economical and efficient employment of available resources. (It
can be both salutary and instructive to develop a fools' project for
the socialist supply of food by Local Feeding Monopolies; to be
justified on the grounds that that is something too essential to be
left to the private market. No doubt under such a system officials
would be directing reluctant eaters to notoriously unsatisfactory
restaurants because they had a statutory responsibility 'to ensure
the economical employment of all available messing resources'.[56])

Decentralizing moves of the second sort provide for the Local
Management of Schools (LMS).[57] Under the 1988 Act every
LEM is to have a General Schools Budget consisting of three
elements: first, Mandatory Exceptions, which are the amounts
LEM's *must retain* for their central services; second, Discretionary
Exceptions, which are the amounts which LEMs *may choose to*

retain for central services; and, third, the Aggregated Budget, which is what the LEM *must pass to its schools to be managed by them.*

One of the most important features of the Act thus is: to make visible the proportions of the total budgets of LEMs which are spent directly in and on the schools and the proportions which are spent in and around the Shire and Town Halls; and thereby to generate strong pressures from below to diminish the former and to increase the latter. On 5 February 1990 Angela Rumbold, in reply to a parliamentary question by Steve Norris, revealed some of the percentages of General Schools Budgets which had been retained and passed on by various LEMs. Many have retained 35-40 per cent centrally leaving only 60-65 per cent for the schools. The most generous LEM was Sefton, on Merseyside, which passed on 76.59 per cent; the least was Newham, in London, passing on only 57 per cent. A word to the wise is sufficient.

Decentralizing moves of the third and most drastic sort provide for the possibility of opting out of LEM control, and thus putting something much nearer to 100 per cent of the available funds at the disposal of the individual schools so choosing. Anyone familiar with the way in which independent (non-state) schools contrive to manage themselves, for the most part fairly satisfactorily, without either direction from any local bureaucracy or much if any advice from any external advisors, is bound to welcome all such moves to bring the management and control of available resources closer to the chalk face.

If and in so far as Heads rise to the challenge of these fresh and more extensive LMS responsibilities, they will surely deserve proportionately increased salaries.[58] And if these are granted, as they properly and very easily can be, out of the corresponding savings in and around the Town and Shire halls, then this particular reform will have created an interest group making it politically at least awkward if not impossible to reverse.

By contrast: since it is scarcely possible that more than at most 200 maintained schools will have opted out before the next General Election, the Opposition parties if elected should find little difficulty in keeping their promise, or fulfilling their threat, to resubject all such insubordinate schools to the vengeful authority of their former LEMs, 'on the first day'.

(iii) All these three sorts of decentralizing moves are measures of a kind which a prudent administration committed to implementing a comprehensive educational vouchers programme by the end of a parliament would be well advised to introduce at the beginning. The present Minister has, of course, disowned any such plans or intentions. But some of his supporters claim that these moves constitute first steps towards 'a paperless voucher'. Certainly it is true that, to the extent that dissatisfied parents are able to remove their children to a preferred alternative school, and if and to the extent that it is also ensured that the funding follows the pupils to the actually preferred schools, then the result will be a system under which all the individual schools are exposed to the incentives and disciplines of the market. They will become constrained to compete to attract and retain pupils. Such a system would be by no means sufficient to satisfy true friends of the voucher.[59] Yet it would nevertheless for us constitute an enormous improvement over the present maintained school monopoly.

The most compelling reason for trying to introduce market competition between schools has been provided by those researchers who in the last ten or so years have found equally well or ill resourced schools, handling intakes with roughly the same social and ability mix, but still differing in both academic and non-academic performance by factors of two or even more.[60] For where in any competitive market can we find firms able to persist indefinitely in giving as little as only half as good value for money as that provided by the competition? Is there, indeed, any known effective alternative: either as a stimulus to improvement for those schools which are at present second rate or worse; or as the discovery procedure for uncovering the secrets of the success of the more successful of the schools involved in such comparisons? It is, therefore, as absurd as it is nowadays common for politicians to denounce a two (or more) class (or standard) system of treatment or teaching or whatever else, while still stubbornly refusing even to entertain the suggestion that market competition is the obvious sovereign remedy for all such inequalities of equally well or ill resourced service.

That the crucial facts are not seriously in dispute can perhaps be demonstrated most convincingly by quoting a restatement of those facts from a politician totally committed to not drawing what is, surely, the intellectually inescapable moral. For, as the Socialist Shadow Minister of Education, Jack Straw is impatient to complete and to tighten rather than to break up the maintained school monopoly. Yet in his article on 'Failing the Teachers', in *The Times* for 20 September 1990, he asserted, without hesitation or qualification:

Study after study has shown a disturbing and gratuitous variation in the performance of otherwise similar schools in similar areas, with similar funding. The greatest challenge to education policy is how to reduce this variation. As one recent study commented, 'If schools were improved only within the current range of performance of urban comprehensive schools, this would be enough to transform the standards of secondary education'.

Notes

1 'Undotheboys Hall', in Cox, C.B. and Dyson A.E., *Fight for Education*, London: Critical Quarterly, 1969. p. 20.

2 Walberg and others 1988, p. 1. This comparison cannot be easily and decisively discounted by reference to underpaid or unpaid nuns. For 80 per cent of the teachers in Chicago's Roman Catholic schools are now laypersons (p. 26).

3 Ibid., pp. 96ff. The same section suggests some of the reasons why.

4 Ibid., p. 95. This book cannot properly be dismissed as 'right-wing' or 'Reaganite', and therefore inconsiderable. For it is a bipartisan production, sponsored jointly by the United Republican Fund of Illinois and the Illinois Council on Democratic Policy.

5 Mill thus has some claim to have entertained here the notion of education vouchers, most recently revived and christened by Milton Friedman in *Capitalism and Freedom*, Chicago: Chicago UP, 1962, pp. 86-98. But its first parent would appear to have been the radical Tom Paine in *The Rights of Man*, 1791. See pp. 263-7 in the Penguin Books reprint of 1984.

6 This is precisely what those urging the establishment of a system of public common (comprehensive) schools in the USA had for many years already been urging as its main purpose and merit. Thus in his *12th Annual Report to the Massachusetts Board of Education*, 1848, which is still regarded as a key statement of the purposes of that system, Horace Mann expressed his belief that 'education...beyond all other devices of human origin, is the great equalizer of the conditions of men...'

7 IV (vii) 7; pp. 794-5 in Vol III of the *Collected Works*, Toronto, and London: Toronto UP, and Routledge, 1965.

8 The sinister title aptly chosen for the most widely circulated work of Skinner, B.F., for many years the doyen of Behaviourist psychology, New York: Knopfer, 1971. This work was also published in the UK, and later Pelicanned.

9 Smith, Adam, *An Inquiry into the Nature and Causes of the Wealth of Nations*, I (ii) 2, p. 27 in the Glasgow and Indianapolis edition, Liberty Press.

10 Compare, for instance, Section 4 of my *Self-improvement and Social Action*, London: Social Affairs Unit, 1989.

11 Quoted by Friedman, M. and R. in *Free to Choose*, London: Secker and Warburg, 1982, pp. 173-4.

12 See, for instance, Flew 1989.

13 For information about some of these programmes see: Scruton, R., *World Studies: Education or Indoctrination?*, London: Institute for European Defence and Strategic Studies, 1985; Palmer, F., (Ed.) *Anti-Racism: An Assault on Education and Value*, London: Sherwood, 1986; and Scruton, R., Ellis-Jones, A., and O'Keeffe, D., *Education and Indoctrination: An Attempt at Definition and A Review of Social and Political Implications*, London: Educational Research Centre, 1985.

14 Compare 'Peace, "Peace Studies", and the "Peace Movement"', in my *Power to the Parents: Reversing Educational Decline*, London: Sherwood, 1987.

15 Thus Edward Short as Minister in 1970, when asked by Mr Biggs-Davison in the House of Commons: 'What consideration has been given to the misgivings of American educationists—for all their experience—about an almost universal comprehensive system?', replied characteristically: 'I do not know of misgivings on the part of Americans'.

16 Compare the 1981 statement of Mrs Shirley Williams, a sometime Labour Secretary of State at the Department of Education and Science (DES), quoted at p. 63 of Flew 1987.

17 Cox, C., Marks, J., and Pomian-Srzednicki, M., *Standards in English Schools*, London: National Council for Educational Standards, 1983, p. 61.

18 Cox, C., and Marks, J., later published *The Insolence of Office*, London: Claridge, 1988, their own full account of this remarkable and disturbing affair. Alternatively or additionally compare Chapter 2 of Flew 1987.

19 Rubinstein, D., and Stoneman, C. (Eds.) *Education for Democracy*, Harmondsworth: Penguin, Second Edition 1972, pp.139 and 140.

20 Hargreaves, D., *The Challenge of the Comprehensive School*, London: Routledge and Kegan Paul, 1982, p. 51. Former Prime Minister Wilson may perhaps have been sincere, even if unwontedly innocent, in claiming that for him the object of the revolution was to provide 'a grammar school education for all'.

21 Ibid., p. 128. On the ideology of the Comprehensive Revolution in general see Shaw, B., *Comprehensive Schooling: The Impossible Dream?*, Oxford: Blackwell, 1983, passim.

22 The new General Certificate of Secondary Education (GCSE), replacing the whilom GCE O-level and CSE, was introduced in response—or should one say capitulation?—to demands of this kind. Among the best critiques are: North, J., (Ed.) *GCE: An Examination*, London: Claridge, 1987; S. Sexton (Ed.) *GCE: A Critical Analysis*, London: Institute of Economic Affairs, 1988; and S. Sexton (Ed.) *GCSE*, London: Institute of Economic Affairs, 1990.

23 It should be remembered more often that *gleichschaltung* —'making alike; or equalizing'—was the central aim of domestic policy for Adolf Hitler's National *Socialist* German Workers' Party (emphasis added).

24 Despite the popular prejudice to the contrary, persistently promoted by the teachers' unions and their political and media friends, there have during the Thatcher years been no overall cuts in state spending under the budget heading 'Education'. On the contrary: in a written parliamentary answer the DES stated that between 1979 and 1989 spending per pupil had increased by 42 per cent *in real terms*. But how much of this has been and is going into the local and national bureaucracies, into hordes of Inspectors and Advisers, and into maintaining superfluous 'places' is, of course, another story. Since most decisions about resource allocation are made in the Town and Shire Halls we should recall Trotsky's realistic warning: 'Whenever anyone has something to distribute, he will not forget himself.'

25 *A pilot test of basic numeracy of 4th and 5th Year Secondary Pupils*, London: Institute of Mathematics, 1977, conveniently reprinted in Cox, C., and Marks, J., (Eds.) *The Right to Learn*, London: Centre for Policy Studies, 1982, and Prais, S.J., and Wagner, K., *Schooling Standards in Britain and West Germany*, London: NIESR, 1985.

26 Stoll, P. and O'Keeffe, D., *Officially Present*, London: Institute of Economic Affairs, 1989.

27 See its third report *Examination in Secondary Schools: the GCE and Sixth Form Studies*, Appendix F.

28 Hobbes, T., *Leviathan*, Chapter XLVII.

29 Turner, M., *Sponsored Reading Failure*, Wokingham, Surrey: IEA Education Unit, 1990. Compare also Chew, J., *Spelling Standards and Results among Sixth Formers 1984-90*, York: Campaign for Real Education, 1990. This compares the wretched performance of sets of British sixth formers with the generally superior showing of sets of materially disadvantaged Zulu children in South Africa—children taught in classes of 40 or more, but actually being taught rather than 'learning facilitated'.

30 Crosland, C.A.R., *Socialism Now, and Other Essays*, London: Cape, 1974, p.200.

31 See, for instance, Blumenfeld, S.L., *NEA: Trojan Horse in American Education*, Boise, ID: Paradigm, 1984, Ch. 10.

32   Lynn, R., *Educational Achievement in Japan: Lessons for the West*, London: MacMillan and Social Affairs Unit, 1988, p. 112 and passim. See also Note 24, above.

33   Wilkinson, M., *Lessons from Europe: A comparison of British and West European Schooling*, London: Centre for Policy Studies, 1977, p. 97. For further relevant facts see pp. 97-103.

34   Blaug, M., *An Introduction to the Economics of Education*, London: Allen Lane Penguin Press, 1970.

35   Ibid., p. 276.

36   Ibid., p. 277.

37   Quoted in Cox, C.B., and Dyson, A.E., (Eds.) *Black Paper Three*, London: Critical Quarterly, 1971. Elsewhere in the same collection (p. 48) the same egregious Minister is quoted as in another speech asserting that the publication of *Black Paper No. 1* marked 'the blackest day in English education for a hundred years'.

38   The value and effectiveness of a programme for environmental education would, similarly, be best tested by finding whether pupils had been successfully taught: not that all the trouble is due to *other people* (capitalists) seeking profits; but *themselves* to eschew vandalism and littering. It would perhaps help both to achieve this reformist rather than revolutionary purpose and marginally to reduce maintenance costs if British schools all followed what is, apparently, the Japanese practice under which at the end of the school day classes tidy and clean their own classrooms.

39   Anderson D., in Anderson et al, *Breaking the Spell of the Welfare State: Strategies for Reducing Public Expenditure*, (London: Social Affairs Unit, 1981), pp. 29-30 (emphasis original). Compare also A. Flew *et al. The Pied Piper of Education*, (London: Social Affairs Unit, 1981).

40   The misdescription of a reluctance to spend other people's money as miserly presumably appeals to those people because it seems to licence the proud characterization of their own eagerness to do so as generous and compassionate. On members of the self-styled 'caring professions' who show themselves to be less than singlemindedly caring by refusing to attend to questions of efficient resource allocation see, for instance, my 'Do-gooders doing no good?', in Jones, C., and Brenton, M., (Eds.), *The Year Book of Social Policy in Britain 1984-5*, (London: Routledge, 1985), pp.225-40.

41   Anxiety about the prospects of such children after the revolution was, of course, one of the golden threads running through the *Black Papers*; though this did not save the contributors from being condemned in Prime Minister Callaghan's 1976 Ruskin speech as 'defenders of privilege'.That these anxieties were all too well grounded is suggested by figures from the Universities Central Council on Admissions (UCCA) and its predecessor. Admission of the offspring of parents from the Registrar General's social classes IV and V from the 1920s and right up to 1961 hovered around an internationally outstanding 26%. They peaked in 1968 at 31 per cent. By 1973 they were down to 28 per cent while in 1978 they began to bottom out at around 20 per cent: 1978 - 23 per cent; 1979 - 22 per cent; 1980 - 19.4 per cent; 1981 - 17.5 per cent; 1982 - 18 per cent; 1983 - 19.5 per cent; 1984 - 19.7 per cent; and 1985 - 20.5 per cent.

42   Cox, C., and Marks, J., *Sixth Forms in ILEA Comprehensives: A Cruel Confidence Trick*, London: NCES, 1980.

43   The figures usually quoted are that, catering for no more than 7 per cent of all leavers, the independent schools, taking boarding and day together, used to get about 16 per cent of all O-level passes, 25 per cent about of all A-level passes, and about 50 per cent of all grade As at A-level. The Heads of these schools are now whispering that, thanks to the substantially lower standards demanded by the truly comprehensive and undivisive GCSE, it has become almost impossible for their pupils not to get grade As.

44   I thank Professor Anthony O'Hear for providing me with these figures. See his *Education and Democracy: Against the Educational Establishment*, London: Claridge, 1991, pp. 6-7.

45   See note 24 above.

46 See Taylor, C., *Raising Educational Standards*, London: Centre for Policy Studies, 1990, Appendix II.

47 Compare Notes 25 and 32, above; also O'Hear 1991, p.8.

48 Compare any of the works mentioned at pp. 13-14, above.

49 To throw still more resources into an industry refusing to provide reliable measures of its output and, consequently, of its productivity is, it has been suggested, about as sensible—though happily not so lethal—as giving World War I generals more troops to send to their futile deaths from the fire of entrenched machine guns.

50 In a House of Lords debate on the Bill (18 April 1988, column 1263) Lord Joseph, who, as a long-serving and at that time the most recent former Minister of Education and Science, was surely in a position to know, described the then state of the maintained schools as a 'national catastrophe'. Compare also *Power to the Parents: Reversing Educational Decline*, cited in Note 14, above.

51 For an account of this 'progressive-egalitarian' ideology, which has for the last twenty or more years been strenuously propagated in most teacher training institutions, and which has played such a large part in producing this 'national catastrophe', see O'Keeffe, D.J., *The Wayward Elite: A Critique of British Teacher-Education*, London: Adam Smith Institute, 1990.

52 See, for instance, Honeyford, R.,'The National Curriculum and its Official Distortion', in *The Salisbury Review* for June 1990; and Ivens, K. and Seaton, N., *Operation Whole Curriculum: A Tangled Web?*, York: Campaign for Real Education, 1990.

53 A figure as high as 40 per cent, derived I know not how, has sometimes been cited for the Inner London Education Authority (ILEA) in the last year of its existence.

54 See again, *Operation Whole Curriculum* from Note 52 and *The Wayward Elite* from Note 50, above.

55 The need for such independent tests of pupil and consequently teacher performance was emphatically underlined earlier this year when, at the request of many concerned parents, Dr Martin Turner (See Note 29, above, and the text thereto) gave standard reading tests to children from a school the pretended achievements of which had recently been enthusiastically publicized and commended in a series of BBC TV programmes. Although teachers had assured the parents that their children were doing very well, properly independent testing showed that a set of children above average in IQ was in fact well below average in reading skill. See the *Mail on Sunday* for 14 April 1991 or Turner's own future publications.

56 Compare West, E.G., *Education and the State*, London: Institute of Economic Affairs, 1970, pp. 13-4, 22-5, 62-4, 182-3, 216-7; and compare my *Power to the Parents*, pp. 97-9.

57 Aficionados of *Yes, Minister* and *Yes, Prime Minister* would scarcely have been surprised to learn from *The Spectator* for 11 March 1989 that the passing of an Act providing for LMS was immediately followed by increased staffing at the DES.

58 The Governors of one opted-out school recently announced their intention to award a thumping and, as I happen to know, well-deserved salary increase to their Headmaster.

59 For some of the reasons why not see, for instance, my *Power to the Parents*.

60 The studies in question are: Rutter, M. *et al.*, *15,000 Hours*, London: Open Books, 1979; Marks, J., Cox, C. and Pomian-Srzednicki, M., *Standards in English Schools: Second Report*, and *Examination Performance of Secondary Schools in ILEA*, London: NCES, 1983, 1985 and 1986; Smith, D., and Tomlinson, S., *The School Effect*, London: Policy Studies Institute, 1989; and Mortimore, P. *et al.*, *School Matters*, London: Open Books, 1988.

3

Vouchers for Schooling

Marjorie Seldon

There is increasing acceptance by academics of all schools of thought and growing awareness among parents and taxpayers that government provision of schooling is neither efficient nor equal in its treatment of children.

Efficiency requires that school-leavers are literate and numerate and able to compete in tough world markets. Significantly Milton Keynes, a town with only three per cent unemployment, has to hold remedial classes in arithmetic for intelligent 16 year-olds before they can enter the Training Centre's machine shop. In other cities school-leavers are not lucky enough to be taught in Training Centres and they are likely to become the nation's unemployed.

The Government hopes that the national curriculum will raise standards, but I do not think it will reduce truancy, already some 25 per cent in inner-city schools. Indeed, it may increase post-registration truancy, identified in a recent study by O'Keeffe and Stoll[1] as the practice of pupils absconding from subjects they dislike. You cannot teach any subject to empty desks. The desks must be filled because the schools are good. And that requires parental power to reject bad schools. Basic subjects are already taught in private and the better state schools to satisfy parents whose children are there by choice. Such schools will be constrained by the national curriculum. Indeed independent secondary schools are already declaring they will not test at 14.

The most effective way to assess the quality of a teacher, the latest plank in the Government's reforms, is parental observation of children's progress. A century ago British parents were well thought of by the experts of their day: 'It is a subject of wonder how people so destitute of education as labouring parents commonly are, can be such just judges as they commonly are, of the effective qualities of a teacher'. So said the Newcastle Commission on Popular Education in 1861. Today's judgement of teachers will not come from individual parents, because in 1991 they have little or no choice.

Many with a vested interest in state schooling—politicians, local government officials, trade union secretaries—find inefficiency more acceptable than inequality. They face a dilemma, for state schooling is *both* inefficient and unequal, but *both* defects can be corrected only in the market where parents are empowered to reject inefficient schools and the less articulate, who cannot explain their reasons, are not elbowed out by the parents who can.

Government reforms in the last 50 years or more that were intended to equalize opportunity in schooling have generally ended as a middle-class bonus. Consider the alacrity with which middle-class parents took up grammar school places after the 1944 Butler Act made secondary education free. Working-class children were squeezed out. The average village child, as Professor Mark Blaug remarked, had less educational opportunity than in the early years of the century:

> Despite a century of state-provided education in countries like Britain educational opportunities are no more equally distributed than they were 30 or even 50 years ago[2]

And the newest reform, the 1981 Assisted Places Scheme, rarely benefits children from culturally poor families. This is the new evidence presented recently by Edwards, Fitz and Whitty.[3]

Every politician talks about parental choice, but the real nugget has yet to be forged. In a state monopoly—and in the last 40 years there have rarely been more than 7 per cent of children in independent schools—the parent is unlikely to prevail over the official.

'Parental choice can be met', remarked the Education Officer in the Home Counties I questioned recently, 'provided the school chosen is not over-subscribed, now or later, and provided the choice is compatible with the efficient use of resources'. But who decides what is 'over-subscribed' and 'efficient'? Not the parent, but the system. The British state school system is the happy hunting ground of bureaucracy where the relatively poor and inarticulate are lost. The inflexible system says: let there be choice—*provided that it suits us*. No duty to alter the school to suit the pupils is acknowledged. It requires the nation's round children to fit into its square holes.

'We know which are the bad schools', said the Education Officer in a university town, 'but we have to fill them'. They are, of course, not filled by the children of the nearby middle-class university *alumni*, many of whom urge state education for the children of lesser people.

How would a school voucher, representing the average cost of state education, benefit the disadvantaged child? I would prefer to give British examples, but in this country there lingers a myth that more money and more political measures can turn bad teachers into good teachers, sink schools into excellent schools, and illiterate school-leavers into sought-after employees.

American parents are not so tolerant or complacent. Their disquiet about the quality of their 'public' schooling is influencing many politicians—from State Representatives to the Vice-President—to support education 'credits', as they are called. And that may be because their politicians are listening to the many academics—far more numerous than here—who are studying the market in schooling.

In Wisconsin, Milwaukee, black Democratic State Representative, Mrs Polly Williams, has successfully campaigned for the enactment of a school voucher programme which provides low-income parents with $2,500 a year for each child from state funds to enable their children to move to private schools. Racial integration is particularly important in Kansas City where the predominantly black population has difficulty in obtaining access to good public sector schools. To give them the option of paying private school fees, black parents are therefore seeking vouchers equivalent in value to the cost of education in a state school. They have obtained offers of 4,000 places from 50 private schools. Here is an example of the role that private schools could play in forging a classless, colour-blind society.

In Britain the Seventh Day Adventist Church in Islington, North London, charges fees for primary and secondary schools. Black parents are anxious to enrol their children. Fees are subsidised by the Church, which would establish more schools if it had voucher finance to assist fees. It could thereby transform the future of many black teenagers in the inner cities.

Professor Thomas Sowell, the distinguished black American economist, recently found that the significant number of American parents who are moving their children out of the state schools are earning middle to low incomes. As in England, they get less from state schooling than the middle-class white children. The good schools are mostly in residential areas with high property values and high housing costs:

> Low-income families, discriminated against by state and federal legislatives, by state and federal courts, make tremendous financial sacrifices to send their children to inner-city private schools.[4]

Professor Ben Pimlott recently referred, in The Guardian, to the voucher as a kind of Right-wing 'conjuring trick' to advantage the better-off by giving them state cash for private schooling. But there are ways to avoid his anxiety. Many years ago Professor Sir Alan Peacock and Professor Jack Wiseman suggested the value of the voucher could be entered in tax returns, to advantage basic-rate tax payers compared with those taxed at the higher rate and to benefit non-taxpayers who would receive the full state-cost value voucher. More recently Professor James Gwartney, in the Spring/Summer 1990 issue of the *Cato Journal*, proposed to give low-income American parents the full value of the voucher and deduct $150 for every $1,000 of family income, so that it would be phased out at $45,000. Back in Britain, Professor Julian Le Grand, in the collection of essays, *Market Socialism*,[5] proposed that vouchers be given according to area of residence, with higher value-vouchers going to families in poorer neighbourhoods. The voucher is not a rich man's conjuring trick but the poor man's magic wand to better schooling.

The movement from state to private schooling is larger than it may seem in the published statistics of the net annual transfer, which conceal the contrary movement from private to state schools by middle-income parents who 'buy' the better state schools by paying the higher housing costs of middle-class areas—and pocket the balance in avoiding school fees to spend on holidays or other comparative luxuries.[6] The true extent of the effect of rising incomes on the increasing demand for private schooling is shown by the proportion of nearly one in four children in private schools in the high-income county of Surrey. As incomes in northern counties rise, a similar trend is to be expected. Parental choice will be exerted by rising incomes into the 21st century. It is only government that slows the process by denying choice to low-income parents at the end of the queue, which could be given by vouchers next year.

The nearest we have to a voucher in Britain is the investigation into its practicability by Kent County Council in 1978. It found that 14 per cent of parents wanted their children to move to other state schools and a slightly smaller proportion to independent schools. All the preferred schools reported that they would be able to accommodate the incoming pupils. Moreover, 72 per cent of parents wanted choices to include private schools even if they themselves did not intend to choose them. No doubt the British, in all income-groups, think liberty in education should be available to all, perhaps because one day, when their incomes rise, they might want to exercise it themselves.

Lord Joseph, Education Secretary in the early 1980s, tried to introduce the voucher but was defeated by political, bureaucratic and church opposition. The Conservative Party, he said, at the 1981 Conservative Conference, did not exist only for 'the rich and the clever'. He went on to ask the proponents, including the organisation Friends of the Education Voucher (FEVER) to meet the doubts of his officials. Its advisers, including 16 economists and educationists as diversely authoritative as Milton Friedman and John Barnes of the London School of Economics and Kent

County Council, wrote detailed refutations of the officials.[7] But Lord Joseph, who knew the case for the voucher, yielded to Cabinet colleagues who feared that 'in the short run' it would not yield a 'harvest of votes'. Political will is the obstruction to parental choice. Other problems can be solved as admitted in the official organ of the Association of Education Committees:

> It would be entirely possible to introduce a plan... merely by requiring LEAs to charge in full the economic cost to parents and issuing parents with vouchers to cover it, cashable at the maintained school or any other.[8]

Now, although the necessity for a voucher scheme has been made more urgent by continuing deterioration in the state schools, the new Secretary of State, Kenneth Clarke, says it is still not on the Conservative agenda. He envisages that state schools can be made so good that parents will no longer struggle to meet the fees of private schools 'they cannot afford'. This is the not untypical arrogance of the politician in power ignorant of popular aspirations. Is it possible to make virtual monopoly completely successful? The truth, now revealed in Russia and other communist countries, is that monopoly always fails with disastrous results adversely affecting many lives. The arrogance lies in supposing that parents do not want to struggle to bring out the best in their own children.

An earlier British Education Minister, the celebrated Father of English Education, Gladstone's W.E. Forster,[9] propounded a view which ought to be much more acceptable today than that of Mr Clarke. He said in his Introduction to the 1870 Bill for the Cabinet: 'Our object is to supplement the present voluntary system with the least cost of public money, with least loss of voluntary co-operation, and with the most aid from parents'.

Mr Forster could not have foreseen that his Bill, which intruded the state into a burgeoning private school system, would be the stone which set off the avalanche that would destroy parent power. Gradually the state reduced the fees for local authority schools. Primary schools were made free by the Fisher Act of 1918 and fees for secondary schools were abolished by the Butler Act of 1944. In the years after 1870 indirect taxation was raised to pay inter alia for state schools and the number of private schools dwindled. Many working class parents who might have preferred an independent school could no longer afford private schooling. That seven per cent of parents, including many with middling or lower incomes, still continue to 'struggle' to pay fees demonstrates their determined rejection of the political plans for equality enforced by the state.

Some think that allowing schools to opt out of local authority control and manage the budgets supplied by Whitehall will lead to a market in schooling without the upheaval associated with the allocation of vouchers to individual parents. Opted-out schools financed by central government grants would diminish the hold of local-education authority monopolists, but there are well-founded fears, based on experience in other countries, that if cash comes directly from central government, the power of the paymaster will be a threat to democracy. Local management of non-opted-out schools suggests that the articulate parent will have more say in how they are run than parents whose chief concern is the happiness of their children but who lack the confidence and skill to make their views felt. The voucher system gives individual parents in all social classes, not only the influential, the power of exit, without waiting for majorities.

Moreover a block grant based on the total number of pupils does not inform individual parents of the cost of their children's schooling. A recent survey by *Public Attitude Surveys* for the Department of Education showed that 94 per cent of parents under-estimate the cost.

Awareness of costs would help to raise standards because parents would expect more from state schools. By suppressing knowledge of costs, state education has destroyed parental vigilance.

The Labour Party would return opted-out schools to the local authority, which would be difficult, if not politically suicidal, once vouchers had been given to individual parents. If Labour returns to power it would put more public funds into the state schools in a vain effort to raise standards. Research in the USA by Dr Eric Hanushek rebuts the supposed link between expenditure and pupil achievement.[10] He found that over ten recent years pupils in the ten states with the highest expenditures scored no higher than those in the ten states with the lowest expenditures.

Competition promises two advantages. First, it would break the state monopoly by encouraging the growth of a wider variety of private schools to meet the differing talents and characters of millions of children. And, second, it could halt the rising spiral of state education costs. Dr Stephen Easton of Simon Fraser University in Canada has calculated that 10 per cent of help with private fees would result in seven per cent withdrawal from state schools.[11] Vouchers would gradually reduce public expenditure as parents supplemented them out of their own pockets.

The school district of Epsom in New Hampshire, USA has initiated a bold plan to reduce the cost of public-sector schools. Parents sending their child to a private school receive a property tax credit of $1,000, which saves the state $4,000 because state school places cost $5,000.

State schools cannot meet the rising standards people have come to expect from the goods and services such as homes, clothes, cars, and holidays which they choose and buy for themselves. The 21st century will bring increasing prosperity to all classes who will also want schools they have chosen themselves. As their incomes rise they will increasingly pay for better schooling. But the voucher could give all parents better schooling for their children here and now.

Notes

1   O'Keeffe, D. and Stoll, P., *Officially Present*, London: IEA Education Unit, 1989.

2   Blaug, M. 'Economic Aspects of Vouchers for Education', in *Education a Framework for Choice*, London: IEA, 1967.

3   Edwards, Fitz and Whitty, *The State and Private Education; Evaluation of the Assisted Places S-cheme*, Falmer Press, 1989.

4   Blum, Rev., V.C., 'Why Inner-City Families Send Their Children to Private Schools', p.17, in (ed) Gaffney Jnr, E.,Mc., *Private Schools and the Public Good*, University of Notre Dame Press, 1981.

5   Le Grand, J. and Estrin, P., (eds), *Market Socialism*, Clarendon Press, 1989.

6   Evidence is in Kent. Although income distribution is similar to Surrey, only 10 per cent of children are in private schools because Kent, unlike its neighbour, Surrey, has retained many grammar schools thus giving the opportunity of good schooling without paying fees to alert middle-class parents.

7   Seldon, A., *Riddle of The Voucher*, London: Institute of Economic Affairs, 1986.

8   *Education*, 28 February, 1964.

9   Wemyss, W.E., Reid, T., *Life of the Rt. Hon Forster*, Chapman and Hall, 1888, (re-published Augustus M. Kelly, N.Y. 1970).

10   Hanushek, Eric, 'The impact of differential expenditure on school performance', *Educational Researcher*, May 1989.

11   Easton, Stephen, *Education in Canada*, Vancouver: Fraser Institute, 1988.

4

A Note on the Oddly Neglected
Example of Higher Education

David Robinson
and Roy Carr-Hill

Introduction

During the 1980s there was increasing discussion of the role which
vouchers could play in breaking up what were seen as major
monopolies in key areas of health, education and welfare. These
monopolies of dominant purchasers (central and local government
and its agencies) and dominant providers (suppliers, professions
and trade unions) were considered to form not only a series of
cosy conspiracies against the wishes and interests of consumers but
barriers to innovation, efficiency and quality.

The public debate with the highest profile centred on vouchers
for school education. Seldon (1986) set out the ebb and flow of
ministerial pronouncements on the issue from 1981 to 1986,
together with analysis of the memorandum in which the Department of Education and Science identified the problems which it
considered 'would need to be resolved before an education
voucher scheme could be defined, and its implications assessed, for
the purposes of education policy'. (DES 1981). He also outlined
the major responses to that memorandum, alternative ways towards
a voucher scheme, and a 'public choice'-based interpretation of
why the debate took the course it did. A good deal of attention
has been given to the possibility of vouchers for other services,

such as for post-school training for 16-18 year olds and for NHS appliances and associated care.

A voucher system is designed to enable consumers to use their purchasing power to direct funds to those organisations which deliver goods and services of the desired type, quality and price. The essence of the exercise of this power is the availability of choice and, in particular, the ability to 'exit' from an undesired service and enter a preferred one.[1]

Among the many problems which tend to be identified in any discussion of vouchers for health, education and welfare are:

- the 'pigs in pokes' problem
- the 'league tables' problem
- the 'honey pots' problem
- the 'crumbling buildings' problem
- the 'special needs' problem

Each of these might be illuminated by considering aspects of a partly-voucher-based service which has been oddly neglected —higher education.

Higher Education

The funding of higher education is partly voucher based, but rarely described as such. The three main components of financial support for recurrent activity in universities and polytechnics are:

- 'block grant' from the Universities Funding Council (UFC) and the Polytechnics and Colleges Funding Council (PCFC) related to agreed numbers of undergraduate and postgraduate students in specific subject areas, research performance, and programmes of continuing education
- 'fees' from local education authorities (LEAs) paid automatically in respect of each UK student accepted on a course leading to an approved qualification—the voucher element
- income from 'services rendered' such as research contracts, consultancies, patents, publications, short courses, and conferences

(In addition, institutions generate varying amounts of their money from overseas students and from gifts, endowments and investments.)

Fees will account for approximately one third of university income for the system as a whole in academic year 1991-92. This is a rise from approximately one sixth of income in 1989-90. Students can cash these fee-vouchers at any of almost one hundred competing providers of higher education. And the Department of Education and Science has indicated its intention to shift even more of central government support out of UFC/PCFC block grant and into fees.

The intention is to make the higher education system more responsive to the wishes of consumers (students) through the use of their vouchers (fees). However, fees pass from LEAs to higher education institutions without the vast majority of students being aware of the nature or value of the transaction. It is, therefore, a rather hidden voucher system with the consumers, for the most part, unaware of their purchasing power. Nevertheless, it is likely to become a much more explicit voucher system, both to institutions and to students, as more of higher education funding is channelled through it. This development in higher education may be of interest to those pondering 'the intriguing question' of:

> ... how much longer government in Britain can maintain tax-financed, politically-controlled, producer-dominated education ... in denial of the increasing consumer sovereignty that is rapidly being asserted in other parts of the economy, where its benefits in raising quality and quantity of output are commonplace.[2]

Pigs in Pokes

The 'problem': *Vouchers would provide consumers of health, education and welfare services with purchasing power. But in order to make informed choices they need sufficient relevant information about the range of goods and services that are being offered. It is cynical to provide vouchers to an ill-informed public. The consumer will be buying a pig in a poke.*

Universities and polytechnics are well aware that, with approximately one hundred institutions of higher education to choose from, it is vital for potential students to be well informed about what is on offer.

The range of information produced by individual institutions is now immense. There are glossy brochures detailing, in brief, the courses and the academic, residential, sporting and welfare facilities of the institution as a whole. Departmental brochures and course-specific pamphlets and leaflets set out precise details of course modules, the staff involved and their qualifications and research interests, methods of assessment, supervision arrangements, exam conventions, field trip and project work requirements, together with information on where past students are now employed and their views on the course, the staff, the department, the institution and the locality.

To support the written material are films and videos which can be bought or borrowed. Departmental staff make presentations to schools, colleges and careers fairs, while every potential student is encouraged to visit the department, with their friends and parents, to meet staff, tour the campus, see residential accommodation, and get a feel for the surrounding area. Great stress is placed on meeting and hearing the views of current students.

In addition to the materials and events produced by universities and polytechnics to promote their own institutional interests there are several sources of external information. These include 'official' guides to sections of the higher education system produced by bodies such as the Committee of Vice-Chancellors and Principals, 'independent' guides compiled by commercial organisations such as CRAC (Careers Research and Advisory Centre), and 'alternative' guides put out by organisations such as the National Union of Students. Many national newspapers also publish up-to-date information on course vacancies immediately prior to the start of each new session.

The shift to more explicit purchaser-power relationships in health, education and welfare services will need to be accompanied by much fuller information about facilities and activities than is available now if consumers are to make 'informed' choices.

Because of the voucher system, albeit partly 'hidden', which partly funds our one hundred competing higher education institutions, potential students are as well informed of what they are 'buying' as any group of consumers.

League Tables

The 'problem': *Just as consumers need full information about the range of services that are available, so they need information about their quality and value. But indicators of comparative performance of health, education and welfare institutions need to be interpreted with more care and knowledge than consumers for the most part possess. They are no more than over simple and misleading league tables.*

Most producer groups in health, education and welfare tend to argue that their knowledge and skill and, by extension, the organisational products resulting from the exercise of that knowledge and skill are too esoteric to be judged by outsiders to their professions or trade unions. There is also the belief that professional and service performance is nothing to do with the public in general, or even direct consumers, even though they pay either directly through fee for service or indirectly through taxation.

Staff of universities and polytechnics are as guilty of this way of thinking as those of any other service organisation. Nevertheless, they also report more openly to the public on their activities than do most health, education or welfare services. Higher education institutions make public the exam results of their students in both local and national press. The Times Higher Education Supplement reports the proportion of 'firsts' gained in each institution and publishes subject-specific 'league tables' of university departments based on the 'peer' views of departmental heads. Results of research selectivity exercises and HMI reports are made public, as are the results of a variety of other indicators of performance and value. Reports of the new CVCP Academic Audit Unit will be published. There is the annual Financial Times 'league table' of employer satisfaction with graduates from every university and polytechnic and the annual Daily Telegraph 'league table' of student satisfaction with their own institution. Every allocation of UFC/PCFC funds is listed in the public press indicating winners and losers.

Potential students of higher education can find a range of indicators of comparative performance. Other health, education and welfare services could well try to emulate this degree of openness in order to demonstrate rather than merely claim the quality of their product and to better inform those who are deciding how best to exercise their choice as consumers.

Honey Pots

The 'problem': *Consumers with vouchers will be able to exercise unfettered power of purchase and, in particular, the power of exit. Any health, education or welfare system will grind to a standstill because consumers, armed with information on provision and league tables on performance, will all head to the 'best' facility like bees to a honey pot.*

Given the amount of information that is available about the activities, facilities, output, and quality of universities and poly- technics, it might be expected that potential students would all want to go to the 'best' one(s). However, in the current system which allows open access to approximately one hundred instit- utions there is no evidence of any mass approach to just one of them, or even to just a small number. Not only that but students are actually encouraged, by LEA maintenance grants, to move away from home to the university or polytechnic of their choice and still the system does not collapse. This must mean either that all universities and polytechnics are of equal value or that con- sumers, given choice, operate with a variety of notions of best and, in particular, of what is the best for them.

Student consumers seem very well able to exercise judgement about the attractiveness of particular departments for a chosen subject. This might be related to style of teaching, areas of specialisation, the balance of 'continuously assessed' to formal examination work, the possibility of an exchange with a linked institution in another country, the size of classes, the possibility of a specific joint degree, unusual options, an industrial placement, a language component, the emphasis on team or project work, or any other features which differentiate 'the same' degree course in different institutions.

Then there are all the extra-course considerations which lead potential students for 'the same' course to decide that different institutions are 'best' for them. These might include, for example, personal affiliations, the availability of affordable accommodation, distance from home, sporting or welfare facilities, size of institution, or the nature of the locality in which it is set.

With higher education being only a part voucher system, the block grant component determines to a large extent the overall shape and size of institutions. As the fee element becomes a larger proportion of recurrent finance then there may be an expansion of a number of popular institutions or subject areas, such as veterinary medicine or business studies, which are to date constrained. Those institutions which can offer distinctive and or distinguished courses with added value are in a position to demand top-up fees which draw non-government money into the system from purchasers, their families, and potential employers.

Experience of our nationwide higher education system provides little evidence of the honey pot syndrome which appears to worry those who are reluctant to place in the hands of informed consumers the purchasing power of vouchers for health, education and welfare services.

Crumbling Buildings

The 'problem': *A voucher-based system of funding for any health, education or welfare service will only work fairly if the competing providers operate on a level playing field. In the real world, however, the ground is very uneven. Providers will have variable infrastructure costs because of their history and their differing size, shape and condition. For example, some institutions and organisations will operate from relatively new premises with low maintenance costs while others will be housed in old and crumbling buildings.*

The introduction of a full blown voucher system in any area of health, education or welfare would have to take into account the fact that provider units and organisations will bring into the new

72

funding regime infrastructures and sets of facilities of varying size, shape, and condition. Many of those differences will be understandable, legitimate and for which institutions should not be penalised financially, at least in the short run, such as inheriting buildings of different ages which require different levels of routine maintenance. Other differences will be illegitimate and with which institutions must cope within their own resources, such as different levels of administrative support or different levels of space utilisation.

Central government, part-voucher, funding of higher education has coped with this issue by its combination of block grant and fees. Variable block grant allocations for capital development, physical restructuring and other special factors, such as the maintenance by one institution of a resource which has national significance—an art collection or specialised library—is coupled with fees for students which are the same for any particular subject across all institutions within the university sector and within the polytechnic sector. The release of polytechnics and some colleges of higher education from local authority responsibility in 1989 has been followed by a clear move to introduce parity of fee value across the binary line, which itself is set to disappear.[3]

The block grant, therefore, levels the playing field upon which institutions then compete for subject-specific students of equal voucher value. Were the system to move toward being totally voucher based then a new 'block grant' or other incentive mechanism would be needed to ensure long term provision of support for some activity which is deemed to be in the national interest but currently out of fashion, such as a branch of engineering or a particular language.

Special Needs

The 'problem': *Different people because of their differing resources, needs and desires will want different things from any particular service. Voucher systems for health, education and welfare services cannot cope with these special needs.*

In relation to any aspect of health, education or welfare, consumers will want varying amounts of the services which are on offer. These wants will be shaped by present concerns and future prospects. In addition, there will be those who because of their background, condition, or situation will need additional or special facilities or attention.

A voucher-based health, education or welfare system does not imply a common value for all vouchers. In higher education the value of fees-vouchers varies according to the unit cost of different activities. The value of a medical training voucher, for example, is approximately four times that of a law training voucher.

One of the key advantages of an explicit voucher system is that it makes clear what the variable costs are of different strands or packages of service. Anyone with special additional or variable needs can have the purchasing power of their voucher enhanced directly or indirectly through tax allowances. In any event the exercise of the power of exit is an integral part of any really consumer sensitive service. In higher education students can and do withdraw from one institution, for academic or personal reasons, and transfer to a preferred institution accompanied by their voucher. The recent growth of modular course structures and the Credit Accumulation and Transfer (CAT) scheme makes the fluidity and responsiveness to consumer needs and wishes much more likely.

Associated with the 'honey pot' issue above is the fluctuation issue which is raised by those who see CAT schemes leading to confusion, instability and a planning nightmare. Again, experience from higher education suggests that students do not shift their course or place of learning on a whim. Those who do change do so for good reasons. With sensitive guidance on course and career choice, students will no doubt take full advantage of a well developed CAT scheme in order to accumulate a portfolio of subject credits best suited to their talents and most appropriate for their futures.

Higher education institutions in general, and universities in particular, have shown themselves very well able to cope with wide fluctuations in student numbers over the past decade. The University of Hull, for example, had approximately 4,000 students in 1975, this rose to 5,500 by 1981, fell to 4,800 by 1985, since when it has risen to 6,300 in 1991 and will in all probability be 7,500 in 1995. These shifts, over a period of declining unit resources, have been managed through increased efficiency, imaginative course planning, administrative and physical restructuring, contractual variations of staff, increased short-term and shared appointments, and other devices.

Conclusion

To enable consumers to exercise choice among competing providers of health, education and welfare services, increasing attention was paid to vouchers during the 1980s. The highest profile debate concerned vouchers for school education. Surprisingly, little mention was made of an already partly-voucher-based service—higher education.

Recent experience of higher education may throw some light on a number of recurrent issues in the debate about vouchers which for convenience have been identified as pigs in pokes, league tables, honey pots, crumbling buildings, and special needs. Further shifts will be made from the block grant into the fees (voucher) component of higher education funding. Together with a raising of consumers' (students') consciousness of their economic power, this will provide further information on the impact of vouchers on a hitherto provider-dominated service.

Notes

1 Hirschmann, A.O., *Exit, Voice and Loyalty*, Harvard: Harvard University Press, 1970.

2 Seldon, A., *The Riddle of the Voucher*, Hobart Paperback 21, London: Institute of Economic Affairs, 1986.

3 Department of Education and Science, *Higher Education: a New Framework*, Cm 1541, London: HMSO, 1991.

Acknowledgement

We appreciate the comments made by Andy Alaszewski, Stephen Kirby and Fraser Woodburn on an early draft of this paper.

5

Liberty, Equality
and Vouchers

Julian Le Grand

Vouchers are an old idea. Education vouchers, in particular, have been traced back as far as Tom Paine[1] and they were discussed in the French Parliament in the 1870s.[2] (A comprehensive list of pre-1980 references with respect to education vouchers can be found in Blaug,[3] where I discovered the relevant references concerning Tom Paine and the French Parliament.) However, they have rarely received as much attention as now, with academics and politicians of all political persuasions proposing voucher schemes, not only in education, but in areas as disparate as public transport, primary health care, child care for the under fives and aid to the severely disabled.

Not surprisingly, the arguments produced by both the advocates and critics of vouchers have been many and varied. But almost every author, ancient and modern, who has advocated vouchers has done so on the grounds that, at least when compared with government allocated systems, they promote liberty or freedom of choice. And almost every critic of the schemes has warned of the damage that such schemes would do to equality: that giving people greater freedom of choice means that they would probably choose to become unequal. (Here I must immediately qualify these assertions and confine them to those advocates or critics that I have read. Nonetheless these are sufficiently numerous to support the claim that the statements in the text are broadly representative of the literature.)

However, in this paper I intend to argue that the opposite may be closer to the truth. Introducing vouchers in many areas of social policy may do little to promote liberty; instead they may replace one tyranny (that of the state) by another (that of the agent). On the other hand, voucher schemes are likely to be more egalitarian than alternative mechanisms for allocating resources (in which I include markets as well as government), particularly if they are modified in ways I shall discuss. Since the arguments will differ from case to case it is necessary first to give some more details about the current spread of interest in vouchers and the areas in which they are being advocated.

The Spread of Vouchers

The growing interest in vouchers is part of the spread of internal or 'quasi-markets' in the public sector.[4] In a number of key areas of public services the state's dual role as a funder and a provider of services is being eroded. Instead it is becoming primarily a funder, with the services themselves being provided by a variety of private and voluntary suppliers, all operating in competition with one another. In so far as the state continues to have a role as a provider, it will be increasingly residual: the supplier of last resort.

Moreover, the method of state funding is also changing. Resources will no longer be allocated directly to producers by bureaucracies. In some cases the state will continue to act as the principal purchaser, with resources being allocated by a bidding process. In others, of more direct relevance to this paper, an earmarked budget or voucher is given to potential users, or to agents acting on their behalf, who then give the voucher to the provider of their choice in return for a specified amount of the service concerned.

Two early examples of this from the first two Thatcher administrations (1979 to 1987) were the development of the Assisted Places Scheme in education, under which local authorities give means-tested assistance towards the fees of selected children in independent schools, and the inclusion of a care allowance in social security payments to elderly people in residential homes. Both of these were a kind of voucher, with the state setting the budget limits for the individuals concerned, but with the individuals themselves (or agents acting on their behalf) making the decision about the way in which the resources would be allocated among providers.

But the really important quasi-market developments occurred in 1988 and 1989. First, there was the Education Reform Act of 1988 which, among other things, introduced open enrolment, formula funding and the local management of schools (LMS). Together these can be viewed as a limited form of education voucher, setting up essentially independent schools and determining the allocation of resources to those schools by the pattern of parental choices instead of through a state bureaucratic process.

The second major quasi-market development was the National Health Service reforms, ushered in by the White Paper *Working for Patients*[5] published in January 1989. Of these, the one that came closest to a voucher scheme was the proposal for General Practitioner practice budgets, whereby GPs with practices over a certain size may hold ear-marked budgets (or vouchers) for each of their patients that they may spend on hospital and other treatments as they choose. (Most of the other NHS reforms are still in the quasi-market category but do not involve vouchers as such).[6]

A third set of quasi-market proposals appeared in the White Paper on community care,[7] based on the earlier Griffiths Report.[8] Here a 'case-manager' would be appointed for each client to construct a package of care for the client concerned, based on a predetermined budget. In making up the package of care, the case-manager would consider bids from competing provider organisations, including public, voluntary and private sector agencies. Again, the system can be viewed as essentially a voucher scheme with case-managers allocating vouchers on behalf of clients between competing institutions, and with the allocation of resources being determined by client choice (as delegated to case-managers) instead of by bureaucrats.

Finally, there was another development on a much smaller scale, but of considerable interest nonetheless: the institution of the Independent Living Fund in February 1988. Again this is a form of voucher, one allocated to severely disabled people for them to spend on care that can enable them to 'live independently'.

All of these changes are of course the produce of the present Conservative Government; many of them emanate from think tanks, such as the Institute of Economic Affairs and the Adam Smith Institute. However, an important aspect of the quasi-market phenomenon is that proposals of this kind are not confined to the Conservatives. In the centre-left publication *Samizdat*, Michael Young (ex-SDP, now Labour) has proposed a voucher system for GPs, to replace the present payment structure based on capitation fees.[9] As at present, doctors would receive a payment for each patient they had on their list. Unlike the present system, however, every year patients would have to choose their doctor, or confirm the choice they had already made. In Young's view,

> ... this would bring it home to patients that it is they, as taxpayers, who are paying the doctors; and likewise to the doctors who would be less likely, when faced by patients who have their doctors' salaries in their pockets, to consider they are being paid by 'the state'.

In the same issue of *Samizdat*, Patricia Hewitt, an erstwhile aide to Neil Kinnock currently employed at the 'left' think tank, the Institute of Public Policy Research, has suggested applying the voucher idea to child-care for the under-fives.[10] The voucher would be given to each parent at the end of the period of parental leave. Parents could then 'spend' the voucher on a range of approved child care provision. The value of the voucher could be higher for single parents and for children with special needs. The voucher could only be spent on approved facilities.

The voucher idea has also been extended to the other end of the education ladder.[11] The suggestion is that all institutions of higher education should charge full-cost fees, and that all students should receive a non-means-tested grant (or voucher) that would cover those fees, plus a generous allowance for maintenance. There is an equity issue here, in that many students (indeed most) come from well-off backgrounds; moreover, many will go on to well-paid jobs as a consequence of the education they have received at the public expense. But this could be overcome by the introduction of a graduate tax, originally suggested by Howard Glennerster[12] and currently being implemented in Australia. This would be a tax set as a proportion of income levied on higher education graduates and collected through the income tax, or, as recommended by Nicholas Barr, through the national insurance system.[13] The advantages of the graduate tax would be that, unlike the repayment of conventional loans, people on low incomes would pay less than those on high incomes: hence any deterrent effect on graduates of taking up low-paid activities would be reduced.

A quasi-market idea that was actually put into practice well before the present Government is the replacement of concessionary fare schemes by transport vouchers. The problems with the former are numerous. They are usually confined to one form of transport (such as buses or trains) thus disadvantaging those who, for one-reason or another, cannot use that particular form (such as those in wheel-chairs, for instance). They are also usually specific to one area, so that they provide no help for cross-boundary travel or for travel outside the area. Also for the authority operating them they represent an open-ended commitment, with little idea of exactly how much they will be called upon to contribute.

It is not widely known, but there is a system of transport vouchers already in operation. In the 1970s a consortium of public transport organisations set up a non-profit-making company, National Transport Tokens Limited. This provides transport vouchers to local authorities or any other authority operating a concessionary fares scheme. The issuing authority buys a quantity of vouchers (in the form of coin-shaped tokens) from the company and then issues the tokens to eligible concessionary travel users. They use the tokens as full payment for their travel to any participating operator (buses, trains or taxis). Finally, the operator returns the tokens to the company, who redeems them at their face value, plus a handling charge. Any surplus from the scheme is shared with the operating authorities.

The scheme has obvious advantages. To the users the scheme offers far greater flexibility than concessionary fare schemes, for the tokens can be used for any form of public transport, so long as the relevant operator accepts them. And to the issuing authority it offers budgetary certainty: they know exactly when, where and how much they are paying for the service.

From this list of 'alternative' voucher proposals, it is apparent that the voucher phenomenon is not confined to the public sector policies of the present Government. The idea is attracting favourable attention from all parts of the political spectrum. As such, it merits close attention, particularly with respect to its alleged advantages and disadvantages. In what follows, I focus on one of each: the supposed advantage in terms of promoting liberty, and the supposed disadvantage in terms of worsening inequality.

Vouchers and Liberty

The argument that vouchers enhance people's liberty, or more accurately their freedom of choice, is clear—at least at first sight. Users of public services, previously at the mercy of a state bureaucracy acting as a monopoly provider, now have a choice. If they find a particular provider is inefficient, unco-operative or inconsiderate, they can spend their vouchers elsewhere. Users will no longer have to depend on the whim or favour of bureaucrats or professionals to obtain the service they want. Rather providers will be keen to curry favour with users and to meet *their* whims.

However, there are features of some of the current voucher proposals that render the merits of this argument rather more opaque. First, it assumes that competing providers exist already in the area concerned, or, if not, that new providers will be enticed into the market in the search for profit. This may be a reasonable assumption for some services in some areas: for example, hospitals in London. But it is not in others: hospitals in provincial towns, schools in rural areas, and so on. In such cases, the replacement of a state monopoly by a private one will do little to increase freedom of choice.

Even if there are no pure monopolies, more subtle forms of monopoly—what economists call monopolistic or imperfect competition—may exist. In a monopolistic market there are alternative suppliers, but none of them offer exactly the same product. For instance, Eton and Winchester are in theory competing for pupils; but the competition is limited by the fact that, by definition, Eton cannot offer a Winchester education, nor Winchester an Eton one. Choice is still restricted—although, of course, by not as much as if there were a pure monopoly.

Against this it could be argued that the presence of monopoly or of monopolistic competition is a contingent, not a necessary, feature of vouchers. There are some situations where it would be possible to break the state's monopoly of provision and to replace it with vouchers and a competitive market: for instance, as already mentioned, London hospitals.

However, in many areas a degree of monopoly does seem inevitable, if only because of certain characteristics of the markets concerned. These include the existence of imperfect information, of increasing returns to scale, and of private monopolies in the relevant labour markets.

First, the problem of imperfect information. In key areas of social policy users are often ill-informed about the quality or other aspects of the service concerned, and therefore cannot make a properly informed choice. In a conventional market this situation leads to the possibility of the exploitation of monopoly power by providers; and a quasi-market with vouchers is no exception. Secondly, the presence of increasing returns to scale means that even if a market is initially competitive it will degenerate into a monopoly. Third, there may be monopolistic labour markets, for which state monopoly can be an important countervailing force. A classic example is the existence of various professional associations in the labour market for nurses and physicians; one of the most important achievements of the NHS has been its ability to resist the power of these associations and hence to hold down labour costs.

So in certain circumstances a degree of monopoly is inevitable (imperfect information, increasing returns to scale) or desirable (as an instrument of countervailing power). And in these cases the switch of the method of funding to vouchers may not lead to any expansion of choice and hence of user freedom.

However, it has to be acknowledged that, even if there are private monopolies in the areas concerned, this situation is at least no worse from the point of view of liberty or user choice than the previous one where there was a state monopoly. But there is a more fundamental problem with vouchers, at least in some of the areas concerned, which may lead to an actual restriction of liberty as compared with direct state funding and provision: the use of agents.

Under the voucher proposals in these areas, it is not the consumers themselves who make the relevant decisions, but agents acting on their behalf. This is most obviously the case with the National Health Service reform instituting GP practice budgets and the Community Care changes involving the case manager. But it also applies to vouchers for primary and secondary education when the actual users—children—have the relevant decisions taken for them by agents—their parents. All of these are what might be termed agent-voucher schemes.

Now the problem with agent-voucher schemes is that there is no guarantee that the agents concerned will necessarily act in the users' best interests. They will have their own agendas and their own interests to pursue. Some of these may coincide with the interests of the user, but some may not. For instance, GPs with practice budgets will have an incentive to encourage patients on their list to take out private health insurance to pay for treatment that might otherwise fall on the GP's budget. Community care case managers may develop relationships with particular residential establishments and encourage their clients to use them regardless of the latters' true interests.

Even parents may not always put the interests of the child first. Anecdotal evidence suggests that it is not unusual for bright working class children to be encouraged to leave school at 16 and get a job in order to supplement the family income. There is also now a substantial literature on the division of income within the family, suggesting that the principal beneficiaries of many family decisions, particularly those concerning resource allocation are not the children, or indeed even the mother, but the father.

A yet more sensitive example relating to the use of parents as decision-making agents for children's education concerns the type of education they choose. This has been brought to the fore recently in the debate concerning the education of Muslim girls; but cases raising similar issues featured in earlier debates over education vouchers, such as schools for children whose parents follow extreme Christian sects or Karl Marx. In such cases, it would be wrong to argue that parents who choose a school that provides an education in line with their beliefs are necessarily putting their own self-interest above that of the child, or even that they have imperfect information. Indeed they may be perfect altruists (at least with respect to their children) and perfectly informed. But their choices may have the consequence that the education their children receives limits, rather than expands his or her life-time opportunities. In such cases, the consequence of the introduction of a voucher scheme is ultimately detrimental to freedom.

Again it could be argued that the use of agents is a contingent feature of some voucher schemes, not a necessary one that applies to all of them. And indeed there are voucher schemes in oper-ation, such as that for public transport already described, where the agent is the actual consumer herself. However, again this does not take account of the rationale for state intervention in many of the areas concerned. As we have seen, that rationale hinges in part on a perceived inability of consumers themselves to make properly informed decisions. Medical care and education (at least at primary and secondary level) are the most obvious examples of this, but a similar case can be made for community care, particularly for confused elderly people or for those with learning difficulties. In such cases, agents have to be appointed to make the decisions on behalf of the user.

So in many areas where vouchers are advocated, agents are a necessary feature. But does this necessarily make vouchers better or worse from the point of view of freedom of choice for the actual consumer than a system involving the direct allocation of state funds? In some respects, it may make it worse. For instance, under both the present general practitioner system and the proposed system of general practitioners with practice budgets the GP acts as a gate-keeper to the rest of the system. But under the old system, when recommending further treatment the GP essentially acted as an advocate for the patient in dealing with the rest of the system; whereas, under the new system any decision concerning further treatment will directly affect the GP's own budget and therefore she will have to act as judge and jury. The patient has lost someone, part of whose job was to fight for her interests, and to that extent her choices are more restricted. The gate-keeper has turned game-keeper.

There is likely to be a similar, perhaps more pronounced, shift in community care. Even more than GPs, social workers often see their role as one of advocate on behalf of their clients, trying to extract resources from the system so as to meet their requirements. But the transformation of the advocate social worker into the 'case-manager', as with the GP practice budget, will mean that the person concerned will have to make the resource decisions herself—and the client will have lost a powerful ally.

Are there ways in which this problem with agent-vouchers can be overcome? One is to argue that in some cases the lack of ability of consumers to make proper decisions has been greatly exaggerated, and that in these cases the use of agents should simply be discontinued. For instance, education vouchers for post-16 secondary education (or perhaps even earlier) could be given to children rather than to parents. Another case is community care. An ironic aspect of the community care reforms is that they replace a user-voucher system (the care allowance in social security payments) with an agent-voucher (the case-manager system). The principal rationale for this seems to be one of budgetary control, rather than a perceived inability of beneficiaries to make proper decisions; if that is indeed the basis for the change, it might be preferable to introduce budgetary control directly, while leaving the user-voucher system intact.

Even in medical care it could be argued that the information imbalance between providers and users is much exaggerated; that in fact it is little more than that associated with many other commodities such as second-hand cars or household appliances, where it is not considered necessary only to allow agents to make the relevant consumer decisions. However, the truth of this assertion is difficult to establish; moreover, even if it were true, the consequences of making a mistake due to being poorly informed are likely to be rather more serious in the case of medical care.

Overall, even if the case has on occasion been exaggerated, there are likely always to be some uses of vouchers where agents will be necessary. How can we guard against exploitation in such cases? One possibility is illustrated by the Michael Young proposal mentioned above for GP vouchers, whereby a mechanism is set up so that users can freely choose their own agents. However, even here there is the problem that consumers will not always have the information to be able to distinguish between a good agent and a bad one.

In such cases it is hard to escape the conclusion that there has to be a certain amount of state regulation and monitoring. To overcome the problem of sectarian schools, the state may have to prescribe standards, content and even values in a national curriculum. To prevent doctors or case-managers exploiting their position their activities will have to be monitored by an impartial authority. The tyranny of the agent will have to be counter-balanced by the tyranny of the state. The extent to which vouchers actually create freedom of choice for consumers in practice will depend on that balance.

Vouchers and Equality

It is commonly argued that vouchers encourage inequality. In particular, they can lead to selectivity—a selectivity that favours the better-off. In the case of education, for example, under a voucher scheme there will be an excess demand for places in successful schools. These schools may not be able to expand to meet the demand, partly because if they did so they would begin to suffer from dis-economies of scale, and partly because, ironically, they might lost what may be one of the chief aspects of their drawing power: their exclusivity. Hence they will engage in rationing devices, such as entrance examinations or the use of family connections: devices that are likely to favour the already privileged. The remainder of the population would be left with 'sink' schools: schools deprived of bright pupils and stuck in a vicious circle of declining standards and discipline.

In medical care, something similar may happen. GPs with practice budgets, or self-governing hospitals, will compete for the custom of the young and relatively healthy, while spurning those who are elderly or chronically sick. In community care, residential homes will compete for healthy elderly people, while ignoring those who are senile and incontinent. Since there is likely to be a greater concentration of the 'bad risks' among the poor and deprived, the latter may end up receiving fewer services relative to those received by the better-off, thus widening inequality.

It should be noted that, even if this kind of selection did occur, the outcome may not be so very different from that under a state allocation system. For instance, under most systems of state allocation of education, place of residence rather than examinations is used as the principal element of selection. In consequence the middle classes move to areas where there are good schools, thus reinforcing the quality of the services offered and creating a virtuous circle of educational improvement, while leaving a vicious circle of decline in the areas they leave behind. Overall, the middle classes have always been adept at manipulating whatever rationing or selection procedures are used to obtain the best service, whether market or non-market.

Moreover, there is an important difference between state allocation and any voucher scheme. Vouchers give actual economic power to all users, including those at the bottom end of the social and economic scale. The latter have purchasing power, and in consequence the providers have to pay some attention to what they want—which is more than can be said under some bureaucratic allocation schemes.

Moreover, the purchasing power of the less well-off could be enhanced by the Positively Discriminatory Voucher or PDV.[14] Here poorer individuals and/or those with greater needs are given larger vouchers or budget allocations. This gives providers of services a greater incentive to take on such people; indeed if the discrimination is large enough they may specialise in the provision of services to them. PDVs in education could be used to give schools an incentive to take on children from poorer backgrounds;

similar schemes in health and social care would encourage suppliers of such care to look after those who need it most.

A difficulty with PDVs is that if income were used as the basis for discrimination, so that in general poorer families received larger vouchers, there might have to be some elaborate means test, with the attendant problems of stigma, administrative complexity and low takeup. An attractive alternative here is to use place of residence as the basis for discrimination, with larger vouchers being given to families who live in poorer areas. The wealth of an area could be assessed by a sample survey of the gross capital value of houses in the area. This would have the advantage of impeding the relatively wealthy from moving into the area to benefit from the larger voucher; for if they did so, house prices would rise and the value of the voucher would fall.

Conclusion

The principal message of this paper is that we have to treat the arguments both for and against vouchers with some care. It is by no means always true that the replacement of a state allocation system by a voucher system will always enhance individual liberties or freedom of choice; indeed in some cases choice may be reduced. On the other hand, it is far from obvious that voucher schemes will worsen inequality. Indeed, by giving economic power to those who previously did not have the skills successfully to manipulate bureaucratic allocation procedures, they may have significant egalitarian outcomes. Rather than a tool for liberty, vouchers may be an instrument for equality; a fact which, if correct, may lead to some interesting shifts in the political composition of both their supporters and detractors.

Notes

1   West, E.G., Tom Paine's voucher system for public education, *Southern Economic Journal*, 1967, 33, pp. 378-82.

2   Van Fliet, W. and Smyth, J.A., A nineteenth century French proposal to use school vouchers, *Comparative Review*, 1982, 12, pp. 95-103.

3   Blaug, M., Education vouchers—it all depends on what you mean, Chapter 11 in Le Grand, J. and Robinson, R. (eds) *Privatisation and the Welfare State*, London: Allen and Unwin, pp. 160-176.

4   Le Grand, J., *Quasi-Markets and Social Policy*, Studies in Quasi-Markets and Decentralisation No. 1, University of Bristol: School for Advanced Urban Studies, 1990. Forthcoming in the *Economic Journal*.

5   Department of Health, *Working for Patients*, London: HMSO, 1989, Cm 555.

6   See Le Grand *op. cit.*

7   Department of Health, *Caring for People: community care in the next decade and beyond*, London: HMSO, 1989, Cm 849.

8   Griffiths, R., *Community Care: Agenda for Action*, London: HMSO, 1988.

9   Young, M., 'A place for vouchers in the NHS' *Samizdat*, 1989, No. 6, pp. 4-5.

10   Hewitt, P., 'A way to cope with the world as it is' *Samizdat*, 1989, No. 6, pp. 3-4.

11   Le Grand, J., 'The middle class use of the British social services' in Goodin, R. and Le Grand, J., *Not only the Poor: the Middle Classes and the Welfare State*, London: Allen and Unwin, 1987.

12   Glennerster, H., Merret, S. and Wilson, G., 'A graduate tax' *Higher Education Review* 1, 1968, pp. 26-38.

13   Barr, N. and Barnes, *Strategies for Higher Education*, Aberdeen: Aberdeen University Press, 1988.

14   Le Grand, J., 'Markets, Equality and Welfare' in Le Grand, J. and Estrin, S. (eds), *Market Socialism*, Oxford: Oxford University Press, 1989.